Jutland 1919

Introduction

By the summer of 1916, the upper echelons of the Imperial German Navy believed that the Empire would win the ongoing Great War, but understood very well that it would not do so with new battleships and battle cruisers. Even so, the admirals still sought funding for new construction, and kept their naval architects busy drafting powerful new ships for the High Seas Fleet.

Across the North Sea, the British continued in very similar fashion, planning for a new generation of fast battleships unlikely to be built instead of the desper-ately needed merchant ships and the destroyers to escort them.

JUTLAND 1919 is a supplement for our GREAT WAR AT SEA: JUTLAND game, looking at the ships that Germany and Britain would have built given the opportunity. The 31 scenarios included here may be played using pieces from this book, our HIGH SEAS FLEET book and the JUTLAND game. No other books or games are necessary. Ship data for the pieces included in this book can be downloaded at no cost at www.avalanchepress.com.

Credits

Scenario Design: Mike Bennighof, Ph.D.
Scenario Development: Robin Rathbun, James Stear
Historical Text: Mike Bennighof, Ph.D.
Playing Pieces: Susan Robinson, Mike Bennighof
Layout: Susan Robinson
Cover: Susan Robinson; painting by Claus Bergen,
SMS Markgraf Firing at the British Fleet at the Battle of Jutland

© 2018 Avalanche Press™, Ltd. • 1820 First Ave. S., Suite H • Irondale, AL 35210 USA
www.AvalanchePress.com

Special Rules

Game Rules and Components

JUTLAND 1919 uses the *Great War at Sea* system rulebook, plus the special rules in HIGH SEAS FLEET except as modified below. Use of *GWAS* 7.0 Advanced Combat with 19.0 Optional Rules, or even better, the rules from the DREADNOUGHTS supplement, is highly recommended for resolution of tactical engagements, while use of the ZEPPELINS supplement is recommended for airship operations.

Circled Gunnery Factors

Some long ship counters have a circle around the primary or secondary gunnery factor. Circled primary gunnery factors qualify as very long range guns (7.61). Circled secondary gunnery factors may fire at targets up to three hexes away. Hits from these guns do not qualify for excess damage (8.3) or plunging fire (8.8). German AC01 and AC08 to AC12 from HIGH SEAS FLEET are considered to have circled secondary gunnery factors. If ignoring excess damage per optional rules, hits from circled secondary guns at ranges of three hexes only penetrate light armor with a second qualifying die roll of 4 or more.

Outdated Engines

In scenarios occurring after 1917, German BB01 to BB04, BB23 to BB28, and all British and German pre-dreadnoughts (type B) have speeds of 1s.

Baltic Avenue

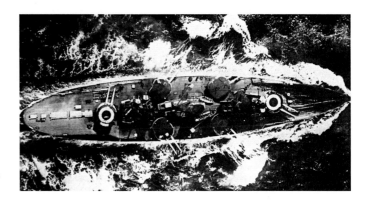

Thanks to the political and economic disruptions of the Russo-Japanese War and the 1905 Revolution, Imperial Russia came late to the dreadnought age. St. Petersburg shipyards laid down the four ships of the Gangut class in June 1909, by which point even the slow-moving Germans had laid down eight such ships with five more on the way.

Those four dreadnoughts saw even less active use than their German counterparts; the High Seas Fleet could easily re-deploy into the Baltic, with an enormous advantage over the Russian Baltic Fleet. Had the Great War begun at a later date the ratio would not have changed and likely would have tilted even more sharply in the Germans' favor.

During his brief time in command of the Baltic Fleet, Nikolai Essen used what ships he had — the dreadnoughts had not yet commissioned — aggressively, even though he had no truly modern major ships. With a fleet of modern dreadnoughts supported by new light cruisers and the powerful new Novik-type destroyers, Russia's Baltic German admiral would have had the means to do much more than lay minefields.

Thanks to the stress and exhaustion of wartime operations, Essen died of pneumonia in May 1915, aged only 54. Had the war started several years later, he likely would have remained alive and in command. A Russian Baltic Fleet with modern warships and a capable commander would have been a potent challenge to the High Seas Fleet.

OPERATIONAL SCENARIO ONE
Sea of Iron
SUMMER 1917

Whenever war broke out, Germany would remain dependent on Swedish iron ore mined in the country's far north and transported through the port of Lulea. While Swedish railroads could carry some of this traffic, the volume desired by Germany's war industries would travel most efficiently by ship. Those ships would be well within the range of Russian warships, but the High Seas Fleet was always reluctant to deploy its full force of modern ships to the Baltic.

Time Frame: 30 turns
Starting Weather: 1 (Clear)
Starting Turn: Allied player's choice

Central Powers Forces

Sea Zone A 51:
Iron Convoy
- BB01 Nassau
- BB02 Westfalen
- BB03 Rheinland
- BB04 Posen
- BB28 Lippe
- CL24 Kolberg '17
- CL27 Augsburg '17
- 12 x S49-class DD
- 18 x fast transport

At or within one zone of Sea Zone Q 50:
Mark one fuel box off each ship.
- BC18 Kaiserin Augusta, Leader Maass
- BC19 Hansa
- BC20 Roon
- BC21 Yorck
- CL60 Dortmund
- CL61 Duisburg
- CL62 Düsseldorf
- DD107 G120
- DD108 G121
- DD109 B122
- DD110 B123
- DD111 B124
- 16 x V170-class DD

At Danzig (Z 48):
- AC15 Gefion
- AC24 Comet
- CL63 Thorn
- CL64 Memel
- 8 x V170-class DD

Submarines
Three submarines may be set up in any eligible sea zones.

Allied Forces

At Revel (N 56):
- BC01 Borodino, Leader Kolchak
- BC02 Izmail
- BC03 Kinburn
- BC04 Navarin
- CL10 Svetlana
- CL11 Adm Butakov
- CL12 Adm Spiridov
- CL13 Adm Greig
- 9 x Ilin-class DD

At Windau (T 52):
- AC01 Rurik
- AC02 Pallada
- AC03 Bayan
- AC04 Admiral Makarov

- PC03 Bogatyr
- PC04 Oleg
- 6 x Ukraina-class DD

At Kronstadt (L 60):
- BB05 Gangut, Leader Essen
- BB06 Petropavlovsk
- BB07 Poltava
- BB08 Sevastopol
- 6 x Ilin-class DD

Submarines
Two submarines may be set up in any eligible sea zones.

Special Rules
Ports: The Central Powers player may use all German ports. The Allied player may use all Russian ports.

Swedish Sanctuary: Central Powers fleets may enter Swedish ports, but may not exit again during the game. Ships within them are not counted as sunk for victory purposes.

Victory Conditions
The Central Powers player receives 10 VPs for each transport that enters a German port by the end of play. The Allied player receives four VPs for each transport sunk. The player with the most VPs at the end of play wins; the Allied player cannot win unless he or she sinks at least four transports or one German dreadnought (BB or BC).

BATTLE SCENARIO ONE
South of Gotland
SUMMER 1917

Russia's fleet building programs concentrated on dreadnoughts, with cruiser support only an afterthought. Many innovative cruiser designs were produced and studied, but the older armored cruisers would have remained in front-line use, at least until they had been proven too dangerous to operate in the face of faster, more powerful ships.

Time Frame: Daylight
Weather Condition: 1 (Clear)

Central Powers Forces
- AC15 Gefion
- AC24 Comet
- CL63 Thorn
- CL64 Memel
- 8 x V170-class DD

Allied Forces
- AC01 Rurik
- AC02 Pallada
- AC03 Bayan
- AC04 Admiral Makarov
- PC03 Bogatyr
- PC04 Oleg
- 6 x Ukraina-class DD

Special Rules
Setup: The Allied player sets up in the central shaded hexes per rule 7.23. The Central Powers player has the initiative and sets up three hexes away from any Russian ship.

Length of Battle: The game continues for four rounds, or until all ships of one side have been sunk or have exited the map per 7.33.

Victory Conditions
To win, the Central Powers player must sink or cripple at least two enemy AC or PC, and score 50% more VPs than his or her opponent. The Allied player must sink or cripple at least one enemy AC and otherwise avoid the Central Powers victory conditions. Any other result is a draw.

BATTLE SCENARIO TWO
Battle off Storön
SUMMER 1917

Russian battle cruisers deployed at a forward base with an aggressive leader would have demanded a German answer; the smaller, older battle cruisers with 11-inch guns would not have sufficed. Modern Russian ships would have to be met by modern German ships, even as the North Sea theater demanded the same vessels.

Time Frame: Daylight
Weather Condition: 1 (Clear)

Central Powers Forces
- BC18 Kaiserin Augusta, Leader Maass
- BC19 Hansa
- BC20 Roon
- BC21 Yorck
- CL60 Dortmund
- CL61 Duisburg
- CL62 Düsseldorf
- DD107 G120
- DD108 G121
- DD109 B122
- DD110 B123
- DD111 B124
- 16 x V170-class DD

Allied Forces
- BC01 Borodino, Leader Kolchak
- BC02 Izmail
- BC03 Kinburn
- BC04 Navarin
- CL10 Svetlana
- CL11 Adm Butakov
- CL12 Adm Spiridov
- CL13 Adm Greig
- 9 x Ilin-class DD

Special Rules
Setup: The Allied player sets up in the central shaded hexes per rule 7.23. The Central Powers player has the initiative and enters anywhere along the south-eastern edge of the Tactical Map.

Length of Battle: The game continues for four rounds, or until all ships of one side have been sunk or have exited the map per 7.33.

Victory Conditions
The player with the most VPs at the end of play wins. The Central Powers player cannot win unless he or she sinks or cripples at least one more BC than the Allied player. Neither player can win unless at least one enemy BC is crippled or sunk.

BATTLE SCENARIO THREE
The Iron Convoy
SUMMER 1917

The long passage down the Swedish coast made the convoys carrying iron ore fantastically vulnerable to Russian surface ships — if those raiders could get past the Germans. In the actual war, the Russians lacked the means to challenge the Germans on the open sea and resorted to offensive minelaying just outside of Swedish waters. With a strong surface fleet, they would have less need to respect either Swedish neutrality or German firepower.

Time Frame: Night
Weather Condition: 1 (Clear)

Central Powers Forces
Heavy Escort
- BB01 Nassau
- BB03 Rheinland
- BB28 Lippe
- BB02 Westfalen
- BB04 Posen
- 6 x S49-class DD

Convoy and Close Escort
- CL24 Kolberg '17
- 18 x fast transport
- CL27 Augsburg '17
- 6 x S49-class DD

Allied Forces
- BB05 Gangut, Leader Essen
- BB06 Petropavlovsk
- BB07 Poltava
- BB08 Sevastopol
- 6 x Ilin-class DD

Special Rules
Setup: The Central Powers player sets up the Heavy Escort in the central shaded hexes per rule 7.23. The Iron Convoy enters anywhere along the north-west edge of the Tactical Map. The Allied player has the initiative and enters anywhere along the south-eastern edge of the Tactical Map.

Length of Battle: The game continues for four rounds, or until all ships of one side have been sunk or have exited the map per 7.33.

Victory Conditions
The Central Powers player receives five VPs for each transport that exits the south edge of the Tactical Map, and loses five VPs for each transport that remains on the map at the end of play or exits the map via a different edge. The Allied player receives 10 VPs for each transport sunk. To win, a player must score at least 50 VPs, and have more VPs than his or her opponent; any other result is a draw.

OPERATIONAL SCENARIO TWO
In the Arkona Basin
SPRING 1918

A modern Russian battle fleet, used aggressively, would eventually have to challenge the Germans in their own waters. As the actual events proved, should the Russians remain safely behind their minefields in the Gulf of Finland, the Germans would simply ignore them and concentrate on the war in the North Sea. Nikolai Essen was not a man to be ignored.

Time Frame: 36 turns
Starting Weather: 1 (Clear)
Starting Turn: Allied player's choice

Central Powers Forces
At Kiel (Z 36):
- BB18 Bayern
- BB20 Sachsen
- BB36 Brandenburg
- BB38 Wörth
- BB40 Friedrich III
- BB42 W. der Grosse
- BB44 Barbarossa
- BB46 Wittelsbach
- AC15 Gefion
- AC21 Ariadne
- AC25 Lorelei
- CL45 Wiesbaden ii
- CL57 Bremen
- CL59 Kolmar
- DD108 G121
- DD110 B123
- 24 x V170-class DD
- BB19 Baden
- BB21 Württemberg
- BB37 Weissenburg
- BB39 Spichern
- BB41 Wilhelm II
- BB43 Karl der Grosse
- BB45 Pommern
- BB47 Wettin
- AC16 Dorothea
- AC24 Comet
- CL44 Cöln ii
- CL50 Fraulenlob ii
- CL58 Metz
- DD107 G120
- DD109 B122
- DD111 B124

Submarines
Four submarines may be set up in any eligible sea zones.

Allied Forces

At or within one sea zone of Zone V 47:
Mark two fuel boxes off each ship.

- BB05 Gangut
- BB06 Petropavlovsk
- BB07 Poltava
- BB08 Sevastopol
- BB16 Alexander Nevski, Leader Essen
- BB17 Chraboi
- BB18 Mostchnoi
- BB19 Tverdoi
- BC01 Borodino, Leader Kolchak
- BC02 Izmail
- BC03 Kinburn
- BC04 Navarin
- CL10 Svetlana
- CL11 Adm Butakov
- CL12 Adm Spiridov
- CL13 Adm Greig
- 15 x Ilin-class DD

At Windau (T 52):
- AC01 Rurik
- AC04 Admiral Makarov
- PC04 Oleg
- 6 x Ukraina-class DD
- 8 x Ussuri-class MS

Submarines

Two submarines may be set up in any eligible sea zones.

Special Rules

Ports: The Central Powers player may use all German ports. The Allied player may use all Russian ports.

Minefields: The Central Powers player may place eight minefields adjacent to German port zones, no more than two minefields along a single boundary. The Allied player may place 10 minefields adjacent to Russian port zones, no more than three minefields along a single boundary.

Mine Sweeping: Ukraina-class destroyers may sweep mines.

Commerce Raiding: Allied fleets with raiding or intercept missions may search for enemy merchant ships on the Merchant Location Table. Sea zones have the following merchant densities: within three sea zones of any German port, 3; within six sea zones of any German port, 1.

Victory Conditions

The Allied player receives two VPs for each primary bombardment hit scored against German port zones, and two VPs for each merchant sunk on the MLT. The Allied player must score at least 30 VPs, and score more VPs than the Central Powers player, in order to win; any other result is a Central Powers victory.

BATTLE SCENARIO FOUR
Trade Protection
Summer 1918

While a minority of German sea officers had argued against Alfred von Tirpitz's battlefleet-centered strategy, they had considered that German raiders would attack enemy — chiefly British — merchant shipping. The High Seas Fleet had not discussed the task of protecting German commerce, but facing a Russian fleet with fast modern ships and aggressive leaders like Nikolai Essen and Alexander Kolchak, they would have to invent a doctrine on the spot.

Time Frame: Night
Weather Condition: 1 (Clear)

Central Powers Forces
- CL58 Metz
- CL59 Kolmar
- DD107 G120
- DD108 G121
- DD109 B122

Allied Forces
- CL10 Svetlana
- 6 x Ilin-class DD

Special Rules

Setup: The Allied player sets up in the central shaded hexes per rule 7.23. The Central Powers player has the initiative and enters anywhere along the south-western edge of the Tactical Map.

Length of Battle: The game continues for four rounds, or until all ships of one side have been sunk or have exited the map per 7.33.

Victory Conditions

The player with the most VPs at the end of play wins. Neither player can win unless at least one enemy CL is crippled or sunk.

BATTLE SCENARIO FIVE
Clean Sweep
Summer 1918

The Imperial Russian Navy had learned the hard-taught lessons of the Russo-Japanese War, and went into the Great War prepared to wage large-scale mine warfare with both specialized mine-laying vessels and minesweepers.

The Germans proved somewhat slower to learn, but knew that the Russian minesweepers should not be allowed to clear away German minefields with impunity.

Time Frame: Daylight
Weather Condition: 1 (Clear)

Central Powers Forces
• AC15 Gefion
• 4 x V170-class DD

Allied Forces
• AC04 Admiral Makarov
• PC04 Oleg
• 3 x Ukraina-class DD
• 4 x Ussuri-class MS

Special Rules
Setup: The Allied player sets up the MS and DD in the central shaded hexes per rule 7.23 and the two cruisers in any adjacent hex(es). The Central Powers player has the initiative and enters anywhere along the south-western edge of the Tactical Map.

Length of Battle: The game continues for two rounds, or until all ships of one side have been sunk or have exited the map per 7.33.

Victory Conditions
The Central Powers player wins if at least four Russian minesweepers and/or destroyers are sunk. The Allied player wins if the Central Powers player does not OR if the German cruiser is sunk regardless of any Russian losses.

BATTLE SCENARIO SIX
Battle of Ottenby
SUMMER 1918

The German Admiralty's reluctance to commit its most modern ships to the Baltic would have been no weaker in the second year of a late-starting war than it was in 1915 during the actual Great War. When Russian battleships started flinging shells into German cities, the High Seas Fleet would be expected to chase them down and meet them in battle.

Time Frame: Daylight
Weather Condition: 1 (Clear)

Central Powers Forces
• BB18 Bayern
• BB19 Baden
• BB20 Sachsen
• BB21 Württemberg
• BB36 Brandenburg
• BB37 Weissenburg
• BB38 Wörth
• BB39 Spichern
• BB40 Friedrich III
• BB41 Wilhelm II
• BB42 W. der Grosse
• BB43 Karl der Grosse
• BB44 Barbarossa
• BB45 Pommern
• BB46 Wittelsbach
• BB47 Wettin
• AC16 Dorothea
• AC21 Ariadne
• AC24 Comet
• AC25 Lorelei
• CL44 Cöln ii
• CL45 Wiesbaden ii
• CL50 Fraulenlob ii
• CL57 Bremen
• DD110 B123
• DD111 B124
• 20 x V170-class DD

Allied Forces
• BB05 Gangut
• BB06 Petropavlovsk
• BB07 Poltava
• BB08 Sevastopol
• BB16 Alexander Nevski, Leader Essen
• BB17 Chraboi
• BB18 Mostchnoi
• BB19 Tverdoi
• BC01 Borodino, Leader Kolchak
• BC02 Izmail
• BC03 Kinburn
• BC04 Navarin
• CL11 Adm Butakov
• CL12 Adm Spiridov
• CL13 Adm Greig
• 15 x Ilin-class DD

Special Rules
Setup: The Allied player enters anywhere along the northeast edge of the Tactical Map. The Central Powers player enters anywhere along the south-western edge of the Tactical Map. Roll for initiative at the start of play.

Length of Battle: The game continues for four rounds, or until all ships of one side have been sunk or have exited the map per 7.33.

Victory Conditions
The Central Powers player wins if he or she scores more VPs, and sinks at least two more Allied dreadnoughts (BB or BC) than he or she loses; any other result is an Allied victory. Neither player can win unless a total of at least two BB and/or BC, of either side, have been sunk.

Massed Fleets

As new and more powerful battleships joined the High Seas Fleet and the Grand Fleet, both Admiralties would face the question of what to do with their older ships. In military terms, the earliest dreadnoughts — the Dreadnought herself and her near-sisters of the next two classes, and the Nassau and Helgoland classes — had limited utility and presented a danger to their crews if exposed to the fire of enemy super-dreadnoughts armed with 15- and 16-inch guns.

Politically, however, retiring dreadnoughts after less than ten years' service would send a very bad message to both the Reichstag and Parliament: that the fleet didn't really needs as many battleships as it claimed. For years the German Admiralty, and their British counterparts to an even greater degree, had stressed numbers of battleships as the measure of naval power. The dreadnought ratio dominated the naval press, and even provided the leading issue in the British 1908 elections. Sending relatively new dreadnoughts into reserve or worse, to the scrapyard, was an admission that they weren't really needed. And that meant that new ones would not be funded.

Internal politics, therefore, assured that at least in the early stages of a naval war between Britain and Germany, every dreadnought would be mobilized for action and probably some of the newer pre-dreadnoughts as well. In Britain at least, shortages of trained crew would have kept the fleet from fielding all of its battleships for very long. Germany, relying on conscription, had lower personnel costs.

The question of just how a fleet that size would be administered, supplied and led into battle, seems not to have concerned either side very deeply.

OPERATIONAL SCENARIO THREE
Seeking Battle
SPRING 1918

German intentions in the North Sea would not have changed greatly with more battleships available, even very powerful ones. The British would still hold an advantage in numbers, so the Germans hoped to catch part of the Grand Fleet and destroy it separately. With larger fleets in play this strategy became more feasible, as the British could not maintain their entire array of dreadnoughts in a single port — Scapa Flow stood at the end of a long, narrow supply line.

Time Frame: 60 turns
Starting Weather: 2 (Mist)
Starting Turn: Central Powers player's choice

Central Powers Forces

Within six sea zones of Wilhelmshaven (AB 31):
Scouting Force

• BB48 Jasmund	• BB49 Eckernförde
• BB50 Sedan	• BB51 Gravelotte
• BC01 von der Tann	• BC02 Moltke
• BC03 Goeben	• BC04 Seydlitz
• BC05 Derfflinger	
• BC06 Lützow, Leader Hipper	
• BC07 Hindenburg	• BC08 Mackensen
• BC09 Prz E Friedrich	• BC10 Graf Spee
• BC11 Fürst Bismarck	• BC12 Manteuffel
• BC13 Steinmetz	• BC14 Arminius
• BC15 Jachmann	• BC16 Zieten
• BC17 Schwerin	• BC18 Kaiserin Augusta
• BC19 Hansa	• BC20 Roon
• BC21 Yorck	• AC01 Blücher
• AC08 Prinz Moritz	• AC09 Königin Luise
• AC10 S von Utrecht	• AC11 Prinz Leopold
• AC12 Stosch	• AC15 Gefion
• AC16 Dorothea	• AC17 Henk
• AC18 Bevern	• AC19 Maass
• AC20 Maerker	• AC21 Ariadne
• AC22 Undine	• AC23 Meteor
• AC24 Comet	• AC25 Lorelei
• AC26 Greif	• CL38 Brummer
• CL39 Bremse	• CL44 Cöln ii
• CL45 Wiesbaden ii	• CL46 Dresden ii
• CL47 Magdeburg ii	• CL48 Leipzig ii
• CL49 Rostock ii	• CL50 Frauenlob ii
• CL57 Bremen	• CL58 Metz
• CL59 Kolmar	• CL60 Dortmund
• CL61 Duisburg	• CL62 Düsseldorf
• CL63 Thorn	• CL64 Memel
• 30 x V170-class DD	• 30 x S49-class DD

Within one sea zone of Wilhelmshaven (AB 31):
High Seas Fleet
- BB01 Nassau
- BB02 Westfalen
- BB03 Rheinland
- BB04 Posen
- BB05 Helgoland
- BB06 Ostfriesland
- BB07 Thüringen
- BB08 Oldenburg
- BB09 Kaiser
- BB10 Friedrich der Grosse
- BB11 Kaiserin
- BB12 König Albert
- BB13 Przrgt Luitpold
- BB14 König
- BB15 G Kurfürst
- BB16 Markgraf
- BB17 Kronprinz
- BB18 Bayern
- BB19 Baden
- BB20 Sachsen
- BB21 Württemberg
- BB22 Wrede
- BB23 Jülich
- BB24 Kleve
- BB25 Lauenburg
- BB26 Lausitz
- BB27 Glatz
- BB28 Lippe
- BB29 Ermland
- BB30 Max Josef
- BB31 Prinz Georg
- BB32 Prinz Ferdinand
- BB33 K F Wilhelm
- BB34 Hermann von Salza
- BB35 Fritigern
- BB36 Brandenburg
- BB37 Weissenburg
- BB38 Wörth
- BB39 Spichern
- BB40 Friedrich III
- BB41 Wilhelm II
- BB42 Wilhelm der Grosse
- BB43 Karl der Grosse
- B25 Hohenzollern
- B26 Franken
- B27 Anhalt
- B28 Waldeck
- B29 Rheinpfalz
- CL24 Kolberg '17
- CL27 Augsburg '17
- CL29 Strassburg '15
- CL30 Stralsund '16
- CL32 Graudenz '15
- CL33 Regensburg '17
- CL36 Wiesbaden
- CL37 Frankfurt
- CL40 Königsberg ii
- CL41 Karlsruhe ii
- CL42 Emden ii
- CL43 Nürnberg ii
- CL51 Würzburg
- CL52 Flensburg
- CL53 Potsdam
- CL54 Göttingen
- CL55 Freiburg
- CL56 Konstanz
- DD100 S113
- DD101 S114
- DD102 S115
- DD103 V116
- DD104 V117
- DD105 V118
- DD106 G119
- DD107 G120
- DD108 G121
- DD109 B122
- DD110 B123
- DD111 B124
- 45 x S49-class DD
- 24 x V25-class DD

Airships
At Cuxhaven (AA 35):
- L30
- L41
- L42
- L54
- L56
- L60
- L61

Submarines
Ten submarines may be set up in any eligible sea zones.

Allied Forces
At Scapa Flow (K 21):
- BB01 Dreadnought
- BB02 Superb
- BB03 Temeraire
- BB04 Bellerophon
- BB05 Collingwood
- BB06 St. Vincent
- BB07 Vanguard
- BB08 Neptune
- BB09 Colossus
- BB10 Hercules
- BB11 Conqueror
- BB12 Monarch
- BB13 Orion
- BB14 Thunderer
- BB15 King George V
- BB16 Centurion
- BB17 Audacious
- BB18 Ajax
- BB19 Iron Duke
- BB20 Marlborough
- BB21 Benbow
- BB22 Emperor of India
- BB93 Captain
- BB94 Elephant
- BB95 Atlas
- BB97 Nile
- BB98 Camperdown
- AC01 Minotaur
- AC02 Shannon
- AC03 Defence
- CL24 Cordelia '18
- CL25 Comus '18
- CL26 Caroline '18
- CL27 Carysfort '18
- CL28 Cleopatra '18
- CL29 Conquest '18
- CL30 Calliope '18
- CL31 Champion '18
- CL34 Canterbury '18
- CL35 Castor '18
- CL36 Cambrian '18
- CL37 Constance '18
- CVS04 Engadine
- 40 x Admiralty-class DD
- 1 x S.184 (S)

At Rosyth (R 18):
Battle Cruiser Fleet
- BB23 Queen Elizabeth, Leader Beatty
- BB24 Warspite
- BB25 Valiant
- BB26 Barham
- BB27 Malaya
- BB96 King Henry V
- BC01 Indomitable
- BC02 Inflexible
- BC03 Indefatigable
- BC04 New Zealand
- BC05 Invincible
- BC06 Lion
- BC07 Princess Royal
- BC08 Queen Mary
- BC09 Tiger
- BC10 Leopard
- BC16 Hood
- BC17 Rodney
- BC18 Howe
- BC19 Anson
- BC20 Sans Pareil
- BC21 Intrepid
- BC22 Unicorn
- BC01 Australia (RAN)
- AC50 Surprise
- AC51 Seahorse
- AC52 Seringapatam
- AC53 Severn
- CL55 Danae
- CL56 Dragon
- CL57 Dauntless
- CL58 Delhi
- CL59 Dunedin
- CL63 Hawkins
- CL64 Cavendish
- 30 x W-class DD

At Cromarty (N 19):
- BB28 Ramillies
- BB29 Resolution
- BB30 Revenge
- BB31 Royal Oak
- BB32 R Sovereign
- BB43 Renown
- BB44 Repulse
- BB45 Resistance
- BB46 Ocean
- BB47 Devastation
- BB48 Hero
- BB49 Irresistible
- CL38 Centaur
- CL39 Concord

- CL40 Calypso
- CL42 Cassandra
- CL44 Ceres
- CL46 Curacoa
- CL48 Curlew
- CL51 Calcutta
- CL53 Colombo
- 12 x W-class DD
- 60 x Admiralty-class DD

- CL41 Caradoc
- CL43 Caledon
- CL45 Cardiff
- CL47 Coventry
- CL50 Carlisle
- CL52 Cairo
- CL54 Capetown
- CVS03 Riviera
- 1 x S.184 (S)

At Sheerness (AE 22):
Channel Fleet

- B01 Lord Nelson
- B03 King Edward VII
- B05 Commonwealth
- B07 Zealandia
- B09 Africa
- AC04 Warrior
- AC06 Achilles
- AC08 Duke of Ednbrgh
- CL17 Arethusa
- CL19 Galatea
- CL21 Phaeton
- CL23 Inconstant

- B02 Agamemnon
- B04 Dominion
- B06 Hindustan
- B08 Hibernia
- B10 Britannia
- AC05 Natal
- AC07 Cochrane
- CL16 Aurora
- CL18 Undaunted
- CL20 Penelope
- CL22 Royalist
- 50 x Tribal-class DD

Submarines
Four submarines may be set up in any eligible sea zones.

Special Rules
Minefields: The Central Powers player place 12 minefields adjacent to German coastal zones (from AB 30 to Y 35, inclusive, including the island of Helgoland, Zone Y 32, and the island of Scharhörn, Zone Z 33).

Advance Scouts: Up to three airships (drawn randomly from available airships) may be placed within three zones of any Central Powers fleet. Mark off one-third of their endurance.

Victory Conditions
The Central Powers player receives one VP for each bombardment hit from primary guns scored against a British port zone. The Central Powers player wins if he or she scores at least 20 more VPs than the Allied player. The Allied player wins if he or she scores more VPs than the Central Powers player. Any other result is a draw.

OPERATIONAL SCENARIO FOUR
Northern Barrage
SUMMER 1918

During the actual summer of 1918, American minelayers carried out the planting of 70,000 mines between the Orkney Islands and Norway, and anti-submarine minefield known as the Northern Barrage. The Germans never attacked the slow-moving minelayers, but the Grand Fleet covered them with battleship patrols just to be sure. Those patrols themselves could become targets.

Time Frame: 80 turns
Starting Weather: 1 (Clear)
Starting Turn: Central Powers player's choice

Central Powers Forces
Within ten sea zones of Wilhelmshaven (AB 31):
Raiding Force

- AC21 Ariadne
- AC23 Meteor
- CL64 Memel

- AC22 Undine
- CL63 Thorn

Within six sea zones of Wilhelmshaven (AB 31):
Scouting Force

- BB48 Jasmund
- BB50 Sedan
- BC01 von der Tann
- BC03 Goeben
- BC05 Derfflinger
- BC06 Lützow, Leader Hipper
- BC07 Hindenburg
- BC09 Prz E Friedrich
- BC11 Fürst Bismarck
- BC13 Steinmetz
- BC15 Jachmann
- BC17 Schwerin
- BC19 Hansa
- BC21 Yorck
- AC08 Prinz Moritz
- AC10 S von Utrecht
- AC12 Stosch
- AC16 Dorothea
- AC18 Bevern
- AC20 Maerker
- AC25 Lorelei
- CL38 Brummer
- CL44 Cöln ii
- CL46 Dresden ii
- CL48 Leipzig ii
- CL50 Frauenlob ii
- CL58 Metz
- CL60 Dortmund
- CL62 Düsseldorf
- 30 x S49-class DD

- BB49 Eckernförde
- BB51 Gravelotte
- BC02 Moltke
- BC04 Seydlitz

- BC08 Mackensen
- BC10 Graf Spee
- BC12 Manteuffel
- BC14 Arminius
- BC16 Zieten
- BC18 Kaiserin Augusta
- BC20 Roon
- AC01 Blücher
- AC09 Königin Luise
- AC11 Prinz Leopold
- AC15 Gefion
- AC17 Henk
- AC19 Maass
- AC24 Comet
- AC26 Greif
- CL39 Bremse
- CL45 Wiesbaden ii
- CL47 Magdeburg ii
- CL49 Rostock ii
- CL57 Bremen
- CL59 Kolmar
- CL61 Duisburg
- 30 x V170-class DD

Within one sea zone of Wilhelmshaven (AB 31):
High Seas Fleet

- BB01 Nassau
- BB02 Westfalen

- BB03 Rheinland
- BB04 Posen
- BB05 Helgoland
- BB06 Ostfriesland
- BB07 Thüringen
- BB08 Oldenburg
- BB09 Kaiser
- BB10 Friedrich der Grosse
- BB11 Kaiserin
- BB12 König Albert
- BB13 Przrgnt Luitpold
- BB14 König
- BB15 G Kurfürst
- BB16 Markgraf
- BB17 Kronprinz
- BB18 Bayern
- BB19 Baden
- BB20 Sachsen
- BB21 Württemberg
- BB22 Wrede
- BB23 Jülich
- BB24 Kleve
- BB25 Lauenburg
- BB26 Lausitz
- BB27 Glatz
- BB28 Lippe
- BB29 Ermland
- BB30 Max Josef
- BB31 Prinz Georg
- BB32 Prinz Ferdinand
- BB33 K F Wilhelm
- BB34 Hermann von Salza
- BB35 Fritigern
- BB36 Brandenburg
- BB37 Weissenburg
- BB38 Wörth
- BB39 Spichern
- BB40 Friedrich III
- BB41 Wilhelm II
- BB42 Wilhelm der Grosse
- BB43 Karl der Grosse
- B25 Hohenzollern
- B26 Franken
- B27 Anhalt
- B28 Waldeck
- B29 Rheinpfalz
- CL24 Kolberg '17
- CL27 Augsburg '17
- CL29 Strassburg '15
- CL30 Stralsund '16
- CL32 Graudenz '15
- CL33 Regensburg '17
- CL36 Wiesbaden
- CL37 Frankfurt
- CL40 Königsberg ii
- CL41 Karlsruhe ii
- CL42 Emden ii
- CL43 Nürnberg ii
- CL51 Würzburg
- CL52 Flensburg
- CL53 Potsdam
- CL54 Göttingen
- CL55 Freiburg
- CL56 Konstanz
- DD100 S113
- DD101 S114
- DD102 S115
- DD103 V116
- DD104 V117
- DD105 V118
- DD106 G119
- DD107 G120
- DD108 G121
- DD109 B122
- DD110 B123
- DD111 B124
- 45 x S49-class DD
- 24 x V25-class DD

Airships
At Cuxhaven (AA 35):
- L30
- L41
- L42
- L54
- L56
- L60
- L61

Submarines
Ten submarines may be set up in any eligible sea zones.

Allied Forces
At Scapa Flow (K 21):
Released when a Central Powers warship has been spotted by an Allied surface ship.
- BB01 Dreadnought
- BB02 Superb

- BB03 Temeraire
- BB04 Bellerophon
- BB05 Collingwood
- BB06 St. Vincent
- BB07 Vanguard
- BB08 Neptune
- BB09 Colossus
- BB10 Hercules
- BB11 Conqueror
- BB12 Monarch
- BB13 Orion
- BB14 Thunderer
- BB15 King George V
- BB16 Centurion
- BB17 Audacious
- BB18 Ajax
- BB19 Iron Duke
- BB20 Marlborough
- BB21 Benbow
- BB22 Emperor of India
- BB93 Captain
- BB94 Elephant
- BB95 Atlas
- BB97 Nile
- BB98 Camperdown
- AC01 Minotaur
- AC02 Shannon
- AC03 Defence
- CL24 Cordelia '18
- CL25 Comus '18
- CL26 Caroline '18
- CL27 Carysfort '18
- CL28 Cleopatra '18
- CL29 Conquest '18
- CL30 Calliope '18
- CL31 Champion '18
- CL34 Canterbury '18
- CL35 Castor '18
- CL36 Cambrian '18
- CL37 Constance '18
- CVS04 Engadine
- 40 x Admiralty-class DD
- 1 x S.184 (S)

Up to three fleets, at or within one zone of a sea zone in Row J:
- BB28 Delaware (USN)
- BB29 N Dakota (USN)
- BB30 Florida (USN)
- BB31 Utah (USN)
- BB32 Wyoming (USN)
- BB33 Arkansas (USN)
- BB34 New York (USN)
- BB35 Texas (USN)
- BB36 Nevada (USN)
- BB37 Oklahoma (USN)
- BB38 Pennsylvania (USN)
- BB39 Arizona (USN)
- CL01 Melbourne (RAN)
- CL02 Sydney (RAN)
- CL03 Brisbane (RAN)
- CL04 Adelaide (RAN)
- 20 x Admiralty-class DD

At Rosyth (R 18):
Battle Cruiser Fleet
- BB23 Queen Elizabeth, Leader Beatty
- BB24 Warspite
- BB25 Valiant
- BB26 Barham
- BB27 Malaya
- BB96 King Henry V
- BC01 Indomitable
- BC02 Inflexible
- BC03 Indefatigable
- BC04 New Zealand
- BC05 Invincible
- BC06 Lion
- BC07 Princess Royal
- BC08 Queen Mary
- BC09 Tiger
- BC10 Leopard
- BC16 Hood
- BC17 Rodney
- BC18 Howe
- BC19 Anson
- BC20 Sans Pareil
- BC21 Intrepid
- BC22 Unicorn
- BC01 Australia (RAN)
- AC50 Surprise
- AC51 Seahorse
- AC52 Seringapatam
- AC53 Severn
- CL55 Danae
- CL56 Dragon
- CL57 Dauntless

- CL58 Delhi
- CL59 Dunedin
- CL63 Hawkins
- CL64 Cavendish
- 30 x W-class DD

At Cromarty (N 19):
Released when a Central Powers warship has been spotted by an Allied surface ship.
- BB28 Ramillies
- BB29 Resolution
- BB30 Revenge
- BB31 Royal Oak
- BB32 R Sovereign
- BB43 Renown
- BB44 Repulse
- BB45 Resistance
- BB46 Ocean
- BB47 Devastation
- BB48 Hero
- BB49 Irresistible
- CL38 Centaur
- CL39 Concord
- CL40 Calypso
- CL41 Caradoc
- CL42 Cassandra
- CL43 Caledon
- CL44 Ceres
- CL45 Cardiff
- CL46 Curacoa
- CL47 Coventry
- CL48 Curlew
- CL50 Carlisle
- CL51 Calcutta
- CL52 Cairo
- CL53 Colombo
- CL54 Capetown
- CVS03 Riviera
- 12 x W-class DD
- 1 x S.184 (S)
- 45 x Admiralty-class DD

At Sheerness (AE 22):
Channel Fleet
Released when a Central Powers warship has been spotted by an Allied surface ship.
- B01 Lord Nelson
- B02 Agamemnon
- B03 King Edwrd VII
- B04 Dominion
- B05 Commonwealth
- B06 Hindustan
- B07 Zealandia
- B08 Hibernia
- B09 Africa
- B10 Britannia
- AC04 Warrior
- AC05 Natal
- AC06 Achilles
- AC07 Cochrane
- AC08 Duke of Ednbrgh
- CL16 Aurora
- CL17 Arethusa
- CL18 Undaunted
- CL19 Galatea
- CL20 Penelope
- CL21 Phaeton
- CL22 Royalist
- CL23 Inconstant
- 50 x Tribal-class DD

Submarines
Four submarines may be set up in any eligible sea zones.

Special Rules
Minefields: The Central Powers player may place 12 minefields adjacent to German coastal zones (from AB 30 to Y 35, inclusive, including the island of Helgoland, Zone Y 32, and the island of Scharhörn, Zone Z 33). The Allied player may place 10 minefields adjacent to coastal zones of Britain, and 12 minefields adjacent to sea zones of Row J, including those in deep water, no more than two minefields per zone boundary.

Auxiliary Minelayers: The Allied player must place one Slow Transport piece (without a Fleet marker) in each of four zones along Row J, no more than one per zone and none in adjacent zones. These are auxiliary minelayers. They may not move in the course of play (they serve only as targets to be attacked or defended).

Advance Scouts: Up to three airships (drawn randomly from available airships) may be placed within three zones of any Central Powers fleet. Mark off one-third of their endurance.

Victory Conditions
The Central Powers player receives 10 VPs for each auxiliary minelayer sunk. The player with the most VPs at the end of play wins.

BATTLE SCENARIO SEVEN
Geriatric Battle Lines
SUMMER 1918

The slow pre-dreadnoughts, semi-dreadnoughts and early German dreadnoughts had no place in battle against super-dreadnoughts, much less the newest ships armed with huge 18-inch and 16.5-inch guns. Little more than a decade old, they had been consigned to secondary duties. But their crews still knew how to fight.

Time Frame: Night
Weather Condition: 1 (Clear)

Central Powers Forces
- BB01 Nassau
- BB02 Westfalen
- BB03 Rheinland
- BB04 Posen
- BB23 Jülich
- BB24 Kleve
- BB25 Lauenburg
- BB26 Lausitz
- BB27 Glatz
- BB28 Lippe
- B25 Hohenzollern
- B26 Franken
- B27 Anhalt
- B28 Waldeck
- B29 Rheinpfalz
- CL24 Kolberg '17
- CL27 Augsburg '17
- CL29 Strassburg '15
- CL30 Stralsund '16
- CL32 Graudenz '15
- CL33 Regensburg '17
- 24 x V25-class DD

Allied Forces
- B01 Lord Nelson
- B02 Agamemnon
- B03 King Edward VII
- B04 Dominion
- B05 Commonwealth
- B06 Hindustan
- B07 Zealandia
- B08 Hibernia
- B09 Africa
- B10 Britannia
- AC04 Warrior
- AC05 Natal
- AC06 Achilles
- AC07 Cochrane

- AC08 Duke of Ednbrgh
- CL16 Aurora
- CL17 Arethusa
- CL19 Galatea
- CL20 Penelope
- CL22 Royalist
- CL23 Inconstant
- 32 x Tribal-class DD

Special Rules
Setup: The Allied player has the initiative for the first round and sets up in the central shaded hexes per rule 7.23. The Central Powers player sets up in any adjacent hex(es). A surprise sighting (7.28) has taken place.

Heart of Oak: No British ship may leave the tactical map.

Length of Battle: The game continues for four rounds, or until all ships of one side have been sunk or have exited the map per 7.33.

Victory Conditions
The player with the most VPs at the end of play wins. Neither player can win unless two enemy battleships (BB or B) have been sunk (not merely crippled).

BATTLE SCENARIO EIGHT
American Standard
SUMMER 1918

While a Royal Navy staffer came up with the concept of a minefield stretching across the North Sea, the U.S. Navy became an enthusiastic supporter of the idea, providing the mines and minelayers for the effort. They also took their turn providing battleship support, which would have to be significant when faced with an increased German High Seas Fleet.

Time Frame: Daylight
Weather Condition: 3 (Fog)

Central Powers Forces
Scouting Force
- BB48 Jasmund
- BB49 Eckernförde
- BB50 Sedan
- BB51 Gravelotte
- BC01 von der Tann
- BC02 Moltke
- BC03 Goeben
- BC04 Seydlitz
- BC05 Derfflinger
- BC06 Lützow, Leader Hipper
- BC07 Hindenburg
- BC08 Mackensen
- BC09 Prz E Friedrich
- BC10 Graf Spee
- BC11 Fürst Bismarck
- BC12 Manteuffel
- BC13 Steinmetz
- BC14 Arminius
- BC15 Jachmann
- BC16 Zieten
- BC17 Schwerin
- BC18 Kaiserin Augusta
- BC19 Hansa
- BC20 Roon
- BC21 Yorck
- AC24 Comet
- AC25 Lorelei
- AC26 Greif
- CL44 Cöln ii
- CL45 Wiesbaden ii
- CL46 Dresden ii
- CL47 Magdeburg ii
- CL48 Leipzig ii
- CL49 Rostock ii
- CL50 Frauenlob ii
- 30 x V170-class DD

Allied Forces
- BB28 Delaware (USN)
- BB29 N Dakota (USN)
- BB30 Florida (USN)
- BB31 Utah (USN)
- BB32 Wyoming (USN)
- BB33 Arkansas (USN)
- BB34 New York (USN)
- BB35 Texas (USN)
- BB36 Nevada (USN)
- BB37 Oklahoma (USN)
- BB38 Pennsylvania (USN)
- BB39 Arizona (USN)
- CL01 Melbourne (RAN)
- CL02 Sydney (RAN)
- CL03 Brisbane (RAN)
- CL04 Adelaide (RAN)
- 20 x Admiralty-class DD

Special Rules
Setup: The Allied player sets up in the central shaded hexes per rule 7.23. The Central Powers player has the initiative for the first round and enters anywhere along the south-east edge of the Tactical Map.

Heart of Oak: No British ship may leave the tactical map (note that only the destroyers are British).

Length of Battle: The game continues for four rounds, or until all ships of one side have been sunk or have exited the map per 7.33.

Victory Conditions
Neither side can win unless at least one capital ship has been sunk. The Central Powers player wins if at the end of play at least twice as many Allied as Central Powers capital ships have been sunk AND he or she has scored at least twice as many VPs as the Allied player. Any other result is an Allied victory.

BATTLE SCENARIO NINE
The Battle Cruisers
SUMMER 1918

Both British and German tactical doctrine called for a screen of cruisers and destroyers to proceed ahead of the main battle fleet. As the cruisers became bigger, faster and more powerful, they remained in their forward position and a preliminary clash of battle cruisers became almost mandatory in any fleet engagement. Not that there were many fleet engagements.

Time Frame: Daylight
Weather Condition: 1 (Clear)

Central Powers Forces
Scouting Force
- BB48 Jasmund
- BB49 Eckernförde
- BB50 Sedan
- BB51 Gravelotte
- BC01 von der Tann
- BC02 Moltke
- BC03 Goeben
- BC04 Seydlitz
- BC05 Derfflinger
- BC06 Lützow, Leader Hipper
- BC07 Hindenburg
- BC08 Mackensen
- BC09 Prz E Friedrich
- BC10 Graf Spee
- BC11 Fürst Bismarck
- BC12 Manteuffel
- BC13 Steinmetz
- BC14 Arminius
- BC15 Jachmann
- BC16 Zieten
- BC17 Schwerin
- BC18 Kaiserin Augusta
- BC19 Hansa
- BC20 Roon
- BC21 Yorck
- AC01 Blücher
- AC08 Prinz Moritz
- AC09 Königin Luise
- AC10 S von Utrecht
- AC11 Prinz Leopold
- AC12 Stosch
- AC15 Gefion
- AC16 Dorothea
- AC17 Henk
- AC18 Bevern
- AC19 Maass
- AC20 Maerker
- AC21 Ariadne
- AC22 Undine
- AC23 Meteor
- AC24 Comet
- AC25 Lorelei
- AC26 Greif
- CL38 Brummer
- CL39 Bremse
- CL44 Cöln ii
- CL45 Wiesbaden ii
- CL46 Dresden ii
- CL47 Magdeburg ii
- CL48 Leipzig ii
- CL49 Rostock ii
- CL50 Frauenlob ii
- CL57 Bremen
- CL58 Metz
- CL59 Kolmar
- CL60 Dortmund
- CL61 Duisburg
- CL62 Düsseldorf
- CL63 Thorn
- CL64 Memel
- 30 x V170-class DD
- 30 x S49-class DD

Allied Forces
Battle Cruiser Fleet
- BB23 Queen Elizabeth, Leader Beatty
- BB24 Warspite
- BB25 Valiant
- BB26 Barham
- BB27 Malaya
- BB96 King Henry V
- BC01 Indomitable
- BC02 Inflexible
- BC03 Indefatigable
- BC04 New Zealand
- BC05 Invincible
- BC06 Lion
- BC07 Princess Royal
- BC08 Queen Mary
- BC09 Tiger
- BC10 Leopard
- BC16 Hood
- BC17 Rodney
- BC18 Howe
- BC19 Anson
- BC20 Sans Pareil
- BC21 Intrepid
- BC22 Unicorn
- BC01 Australia (RAN)
- AC50 Surprise
- AC51 Seahorse
- AC52 Seringapatam
- AC53 Severn
- CL55 Danae
- CL56 Dragon
- CL57 Dauntless
- CL58 Delhi
- CL59 Dunedin
- CL63 Hawkins
- CL64 Cavendish
- 30 x W-class DD

Setup: The Allied player enters anywhere along the North-East edge of the Tactical Map. The Central Powers player enters anywhere along the South-West edge of the Tactical Map. Roll to determine initiative before the start of play.

Heart of Oak: No British ship may leave the tactical map.

Length of Battle: The game continues for eight rounds, or until all ships of one side have been sunk or have exited the map per 7.33.

Victory Conditions
The Central Powers player wins if he or she scores 100 more VPs than the Allied Player. The Allied Player wins if he or she scores more VPs than the Central Powers player. Any other result is a draw. Neither player can win unless at least two enemy BB and/or BC have been sunk before the end of play.

BATTLE SCENARIO TEN
A Single Afternoon
SUMMER 1918

Jellicoe was the only man on either side who could lose the war in an afternoon.
— Winston Churchill

Like most Churchill quotes, the above statement doesn't exactly reflect reality; Sir John Jellicoe might have lost a fleet battle to the Germans, but the war would continue regardless of the outcome in the North Sea. That didn't mean that the sailors would fight any less hard when the moment came.

Time Frame: Daylight
Weather Condition: 1 (Clear)

Central Powers Forces
Scouting Force
- BB48 Jasmund
- BB49 Eckernförde

- BB50 Sedan
- BB51 Gravelotte
- BC01 von der Tann
- BC02 Moltke
- BC03 Goeben
- BC04 Seydlitz
- BC05 Derfflinger
- BC06 Lützow, Leader Hipper
- BC07 Hindenburg
- BC08 Mackensen
- BC09 Prz E Friedrich
- BC10 Graf Spee
- BC11 Fürst Bismarck
- BC12 Manteuffel
- BC13 Steinmetz
- BC14 Arminius
- BC15 Jachmann
- BC16 Zieten
- BC17 Schwerin
- BC18 Kaiserin Augusta
- BC19 Hansa
- BC20 Roon
- BC21 Yorck
- AC01 Blücher
- AC08 Prinz Moritz
- AC09 Königin Luise
- AC10 S von Utrecht
- AC11 Prinz Leopold
- AC12 Stosch
- AC15 Gefion
- AC16 Dorothea
- AC17 Henk
- AC18 Bevern
- AC19 Maass
- AC20 Maerker
- AC21 Ariadne
- AC22 Undine
- AC23 Meteor
- AC24 Comet
- AC25 Lorelei
- AC26 Greif
- CL38 Brummer
- CL39 Bremse
- CL44 Cöln ii
- CL45 Wiesbaden ii
- CL46 Dresden ii
- CL47 Magdeburg ii
- CL48 Leipzig ii
- CL49 Rostock ii
- CL50 Frauenlob ii
- CL57 Bremen
- CL58 Metz
- CL59 Kolmar
- CL60 Dortmund
- CL61 Duisburg
- CL62 Düsseldorf
- CL63 Thorn
- CL64 Memel
- 30 x V170-class DD
- 30 x S49-class DD

High Seas Fleet
- BB01 Nassau
- BB02 Westfalen
- BB03 Rheinland
- BB04 Posen
- BB05 Helgoland
- BB06 Ostfriesland
- BB07 Thüringen
- BB08 Oldenburg
- BB09 Kaiser
- BB10 Friedrich der Grosse
- BB11 Kaiserin
- BB12 König Albert
- BB13 Przrgnt Luitpold
- BB14 König
- BB15 G Kurfürst
- BB16 Markgraf
- BB17 Kronprinz
- BB18 Bayern
- BB19 Baden
- BB20 Sachsen
- BB21 Württemberg
- BB22 Wrede
- BB23 Jülich
- BB24 Kleve
- BB25 Lauenburg
- BB26 Lausitz
- BB27 Glatz
- BB28 Lippe
- BB29 Ermland
- BB30 Max Josef
- BB31 Prinz Georg
- BB32 Prinz Ferdinand
- BB33 K F Wilhelm
- BB34 Hermann von Salza
- BB35 Fritigern
- BB36 Brandenburg
- BB37 Weissenburg
- BB38 Wörth
- BB39 Spichern
- BB40 Friedrich III

- BB41 Wilhelm II
- BB42 Wilhelm der Grosse
- BB43 Karl der Grosse
- B25 Hohenzollern
- B26 Franken
- B27 Anhalt
- B28 Waldeck
- B29 Rheinpfalz
- CL24 Kolberg '17
- CL27 Augsburg '17
- CL29 Strassburg '15
- CL30 Stralsund '16
- CL32 Graudenz '15
- CL33 Regensburg '17
- CL36 Wiesbaden
- CL37 Frankfurt
- CL40 Königsberg ii
- CL41 Karlsruhe ii
- CL42 Emden ii
- CL43 Nürnberg ii
- CL51 Würzburg
- CL52 Flensburg
- CL53 Potsdam
- CL54 Göttingen
- CL55 Freiburg
- CL56 Konstanz
- DD100 S113
- DD101 S114
- DD102 S115
- DD103 V116
- DD104 V117
- DD105 V118
- DD106 G119
- DD107 G120
- DD108 G121
- DD109 B122
- DD110 B123
- DD111 B124
- 45 x S49-class DD
- 24 x V25-class DD

Allied Forces
Battle Cruiser Fleet
- BB23 Queen Elizabeth, Leader Beatty
- BB24 Warspite
- BB25 Valiant
- BB26 Barham
- BB27 Malaya
- BB96 King Henry V
- BC01 Indomitable
- BC02 Inflexible
- BC03 Indefatigable
- BC04 New Zealand
- BC05 Invincible
- BC06 Lion
- BC07 Princess Royal
- BC08 Queen Mary
- BC09 Tiger
- BC10 Leopard
- BC16 Hood
- BC17 Rodney
- BC18 Howe
- BC19 Anson
- BC20 Sans Pareil
- BC21 Intrepid
- BC22 Unicorn
- BC01 Australia (RAN)
- AC50 Surprise
- AC51 Seahorse
- AC52 Seringapatam
- AC53 Severn
- CL55 Danae
- CL56 Dragon
- CL57 Dauntless
- CL58 Delhi
- CL59 Dunedin
- CL63 Hawkins
- CL64 Cavendish
- 30 x W-class DD

Grand Fleet, Northern Wing
- BB01 Dreadnought
- BB02 Superb
- BB03 Temeraire
- BB04 Bellerophon
- BB05 Collingwood
- BB06 St. Vincent
- BB07 Vanguard
- BB08 Neptune
- BB09 Colossus
- BB10 Hercules
- BB11 Conqueror
- BB12 Monarch
- BB13 Orion
- BB14 Thunderer
- BB15 King George V
- BB16 Centurion
- BB17 Audacious
- BB18 Ajax

- BB19 Iron Duke
- BB20 Marlborough
- BB21 Benbow
- BB22 Emperor of India
- BB93 Captain
- BB94 Elephant
- BB95 Atlas
- BB97 Nile
- BB98 Camperdown
- BB28 Delaware (USN)
- BB29 N Dakota (USN)
- BB30 Florida (USN)
- BB31 Utah (USN)
- BB32 Wyoming (USN)
- BB33 Arkansas (USN)
- BB34 New York (USN)
- BB35 Texas (USN)
- BB36 Nevada (USN)
- BB37 Oklahoma (USN)
- BB38 Pennsylvania (USN)
- BB39 Arizona (USN)
- AC01 Minotaur
- AC02 Shannon
- AC03 Defence
- CL24 Cordelia '18
- CL25 Comus '18
- CL26 Caroline '18
- CL27 Carysfort '18
- CL28 Cleopatra '18
- CL29 Conquest '18
- CL30 Calliope '18
- CL31 Champion '18
- CL34 Canterbury '18
- CL35 Castor '18
- CL36 Cambrian '18
- CL37 Constance '18
- CL01 Melbrne (RAN)
- CL02 Sydney (RAN)
- CL03 Brisbane (RAN)
- CL04 Adelaide (RAN)
- 40 x Admiralty-class DD

Grand Fleet, Southern Wing
- BB28 Ramillies
- BB29 Resolution
- BB30 Revenge
- BB31 Royal Oak
- BB32 R Sovereign
- BB43 Renown
- BB44 Repulse
- BB45 Resistance
- BB46 Ocean
- BB47 Devastation
- BB48 Hero
- BB49 Irresistible
- CL38 Centaur
- CL39 Concord
- CL40 Calypso
- CL41 Caradoc
- CL42 Cassandra
- CL43 Caledon
- CL44 Ceres
- CL45 Cardiff
- CL46 Curacoa
- CL47 Coventry
- CL48 Curlew
- CL50 Carlisle
- CL51 Calcutta
- CL52 Cairo
- CL53 Colombo
- CL54 Capetown
- 12 x W-class DD
- 60 x Admiralty-class DD

Channel Fleet
- B01 Lord Nelson
- B02 Agamemnon
- B03 King Edward VII
- B04 Dominion
- B05 Commonwealth
- B06 Hindustan
- B07 Zealandia
- B08 Hibernia
- B09 Africa
- B10 Britannia
- AC04 Warrior
- AC05 Natal
- AC06 Achilles
- AC07 Cochrane
- AC08 Duke of Ednbrgh
- CL16 Aurora
- CL17 Arethusa
- CL18 Undaunted
- CL19 Galatea
- CL20 Penelope
- CL21 Phaeton
- CL22 Royalist
- CL23 Inconstant
- 50 x Tribal-class DD

Special Rules
Initiative: Roll to determine initiative before the start of play.

Central Powers Setup and Reinforcements: The Scouting Force enters anywhere along the South-East edge of the Tactical Map. The High Seas Fleet enters at the start of the third round, anywhere along the South-East edge of the Tactical Map.

Allied Setup and Reinforcements: The Battle Cruiser Fleet enters anywhere along the North-West edge of the Tactical Map.
- At the end of the first round, roll one die. On a result of 3 through 6, the Grand Fleet Northern Wing enters anywhere along the North-West edge of the Tactical Map. If these ships do not enter, roll again at the end of the second round and add one to the result. If these ships still do not enter, they will automatically enter at the start of the fourth round.
- At the end of the second round, roll one die (in addition to that rolled for the Northern Wing). On a result of 3 through 6, the Grand Fleet Southern Wing enters anywhere along the North-West edge of the Tactical Map. If these ships do not enter, roll again at the end of the third round and add one to the result. If these ships still do not enter, they will automatically enter at the start of the fifth round.
- At the end of the fourth round, roll one die. On a result of 4 through 6, the Channel Fleet enters anywhere along the South-West edge of the Tactical Map. If these ships do not enter, roll again at the end of the fifth round and add one to the result. If these ships do not enter, roll again at the end of the sixth round and add two to the result. If these ships still do not enter, they will automatically enter at the start of the eighth round.

Heart of Oak: No British ship may leave the tactical map.

Length of Battle: The game continues for twelve rounds, or until all ships of one side have been sunk or have exited the map per 7.33.

Victory Conditions
The player with the most VPs at the end of play wins. Neither player can win unless at least six enemy BB and/or BC have been sunk before the end of play.

Super Dreadnoughts

Britain's Grand Fleet held a substantial edge over the Germans in terms of dreadnought battleships and battlecruisers, fielding more than half again as many heavy ships as the High Seas Fleet. But while the edge in dreadnoughts hovered somewhere around 1.75:1, the Royal Navy totaled three times the manpower of the Imperial Navy.

Royal Navy ratings were volunteers, paid considerably more than the conscripts who manned German ships. That made the Grand Fleet far more expensive to man, and raised the possibility that Britain might run out of jolly tars before the Germans grew tired of building battleships. Tax resistance by wealthy Germans brought an end to the brief era of heavy naval spending before that came to pass, and Britain found the crews to mobilize the vast fleet of aged, obsolete pre-dreadnoughts as well as all of her modern ships.

On the German side of the North Sea, the Admiralty expressed concern that the earliest dreadnoughts, let alone the pre-dreadnoughts, were no longer capable of operating as first-line units. These should be retired, the admirals in charge of choosing new ship designs argued, and replaced with new, bigger ships armed with bigger guns and powered by turbines rather than the reciprocating engines that drove the earliest dreadnoughts.

Between manning problems and obsolescence, a Great War that started later (or lasted longer) could have seen a clash between fewer but far more powerful ships.

OPERATIONAL SCENARIO FIVE
East Coast Express
SUMMER 1919

In the actual Great War, bombardments of England's eastern seaboard caused a great deal of outrage and a small amount of damage, but did reliably bring the Grand Fleet out of their Scottish bases seeking battle. That dynamic would be in equal force in a war that began a few years later, with faster ships (and more of them) making an encounter even more likely.

> **Time Frame:** 30 turns
> **Starting Weather:** 1 (Clear)
> **Starting Turn:** Allied player's choice

Central Powers Forces
Within ten sea zones of Wilhelmshaven (AB 31):

A German torpedo boat cuts through the battle line.

Scouting Force
- BC05 Derfflinger
- BC06 Lützow, Leader Hipper
- BC07 Hindenburg   • BC17 Schwerin
- AC15 Gefion   • AC16 Dorothea
- AC17 Henk   • AC18 Bevern
- AC19 Maass   • AC20 Maerker
- CL38 Brummer   • CL39 Bremse
- CL63 Thorn   • CL64 Memel
- 20 x V170-class DD

Within six sea zones of Wilhelmshaven (AB 31):
Raiding Force
- BB48 Jasmund, Leader Souchon
- BB49 Eckernförde   • BB50 Sedan
- BB51 Gravelotte   • BC08 Mackensen
- BC09 Prz E Friedrich   • BC10 Graf Spee
- BC11 Fürst Bismarck   • BC12 Manteuffel
- BC13 Steinmetz   • BC14 Arminius
- BC18 K Augusta   • BC19 Hansa
- BC20 Roon   • BC21 Yorck
- BC22 Victoria Louise   • BC23 Hertha
- BC24 Freya   • BC25 Vineta
- AC21 Ariadne   • AC22 Undine
- AC23 Meteor   • AC24 Comet
- AC25 Lorelei   • AC26 Greif
- CL44 Cöln ii   • CL45 Wiesbaden ii
- CL46 Dresden ii   • CL47 Magdeburg ii
- CL48 Leipzig ii   • CL49 Rostock ii
- CL50 Frauenlob ii   • CL57 Bremen
- CL58 Metz   • CL59 Kolmar
- CL60 Dortmund   • CL61 Duisburg
- CL62 Düsseldorf   • 30 x S49-class DD

Within one sea zone of Wilhelmshaven (AB 31):
Support Force
- BB18 Bayern
- BB19 Baden
- BB20 Sachsen
- BB21 Württemberg
- BB31 Prinz Georg
- BB32 Prinz Ferdinand
- BB33 K F Wilhelm
- BB34 Hermann von Salza
- BB35 Fritigern
- BB36 Brandenburg
- BB37 Weissenburg
- BB38 Wörth
- BB39 Spichern
- BB40 Friedrich III
- BB41 Wilhelm II
- BB42 Wilhelm der Grosse
- BB43 Karl der Grosse
- BB44 Barbarossa
- BB45 Pommern
- BB46 Wittelsbach
- BB47 Wettin
- AC01 Blücher
- AC08 Prinz Moritz
- AC09 Königin Luise
- AC10 S von Utrecht
- AC11 Prinz Leopold
- AC12 Stosch
- CL32 Graudenz '15
- CL33 Regensburg '17
- CL36 Wiesbaden
- CL37 Frankfurt
- CL40 Königsberg ii
- CL41 Karlsruhe ii
- CL42 Emden ii
- CL43 Nürnberg ii
- CL53 Potsdam
- CL54 Göttingen
- CL55 Freiburg
- CL56 Konstanz
- DD100 S113
- DD101 S114
- DD102 S115
- DD103 V116
- DD104 V117
- DD105 V118
- DD106 G119
- DD107 G120
- DD108 G121
- DD109 B122
- DD110 B123
- DD111 B124
- 36 x S49-class DD

Airships

At Cuxhaven (AA 35):
- L30
- L41
- L42
- L54
- L56
- L60
- L61

Submarines

Twelve submarines may be set up in any eligible sea zones.

Allied Forces

At Rosyth (R 18):
Battle Cruiser Fleet
- BB23 Queen Elizabeth, Leader Beatty
- BB24 Warspite
- BB25 Valiant
- BB26 Barham
- BB27 Malaya
- BB96 King Henry V
- BC06 Lion
- BC07 Princess Royal
- BC08 Queen Mary
- BC09 Tiger
- BC10 Leopard
- BC16 Hood
- BC17 Rodney
- BC18 Howe
- BC19 Anson
- BC20 Sans Pareil
- BC22 Unicorn
- AC50 Surprise
- AC51 Seahorse
- AC52 Seringapatam
- AC53 Severn
- CL55 Danae
- CL56 Dragon
- CL57 Dauntless
- CL58 Delhi
- CL59 Dunedin
- CL63 Hawkins
- CL64 Cavendish
- 30 x W-class DD

At Cromarty (N 19):
- BB11 Conqueror
- BB12 Monarch
- BB13 Orion
- BB14 Thunderer
- BB15 King George V
- BB16 Centurion
- BB17 Audacious
- BB18 Ajax
- BB19 Iron Duke
- BB20 Marlborough
- BB21 Benbow
- BB22 Emperor of India
- BB28 Ramillies
- BB29 Resolution
- BB30 Revenge
- BB31 Royal Oak
- BB32 R Sovereign
- BB43 Renown
- BB44 Repulse
- BB45 Resistance
- BB46 Ocean
- BB47 Devastation
- BB48 Hero
- BB49 Irresistible
- BB50 Nemesis
- BB51 Retribution
- BB52 Powerful
- BB53 Terrible
- CL38 Centaur
- CL39 Concord
- CL40 Calypso
- CL41 Caradoc
- CL42 Cassandra
- CL43 Caledon
- CL44 Ceres
- CL45 Cardiff
- CL46 Curacoa
- CL47 Coventry
- CL48 Curlew
- CL50 Carlisle
- CL51 Calcutta
- CL52 Cairo
- CL53 Colombo
- CL54 Capetown
- CVS03 Riviera
- CVS04 Engadine
- 1 x S.184 (S)
- 1 x S.184 (S)
- 12 x W-class DD
- 70 x Admiralty-class DD

Submarines

Three submarines may be set up in any eligible sea zones.

Special Rules

Minefields: The Central Powers player place 10 minefields adjacent to German coastal zones (from AB 30 to Y 35, inclusive, including the island of Helgoland, Zone Y 32, and the island of Scharhörn, Zone Z 33). The Allied player may place eight minefields in or adjacent to any British coastal zones.

Straits of Dover: Central Powers ships may not enter zones AF 22 or AG 23 due to numerous minefields.

Advance Scouts: Up to three airships (drawn randomly from available airships) may be placed within three zones of any Central Powers fleet. Mark off one-third of their endurance.

Victory Conditions

The Central Powers player receives two VPs for each coastal zone of Great Britain that suffers at least two bombardment hits from primary guns, and one VP for each (non-decoy) fleet that ends a turn within two sea zones of a British port. To win, a player must sink or cripple at least three enemy BB or BC, and score more VPs than his or her opponent; any other result is a draw.

OPERATIONAL SCENARIO SIX
Northern Patrol
SUMMER 1919

From 1904, British war plans had assumed that in case of war with Germany the fleet would take up a distant blockade of Germany. To enforce the blockade against German merchant shipping, older cruisers would take up the so-called "Northern Patrol" between the northern tip of Scotland and the coast of Norway. Returning German merchant ships would have to make their way past them.

Time Frame: 70 turns
Starting Weather: 3 (Fog)
Starting Turn: Central Powers player's choice

Central Powers Forces
Within twelve sea zones of Wilhelmshaven (AB 31):
Long-Range Escort Force
• BC05 Derfflinger
• BC06 Lützow, Leader Hipper
• BC07 Hindenburg
• BC17 Schwerin
• AC15 Gefion
• AC16 Dorothea
• AC18 Bevern
• CL63 Thorn
• CL64 Memel

Within eight sea zones of Wilhelmshaven (AB 31):
Scouting Force
• BB48 Jasmund, Leader Souchon
• BB49 Eckernförde
• BB50 Sedan
• BB51 Gravelotte
• BC08 Mackensen
• BC09 Prz E Friedrich
• BC10 Graf Spee
• BC11 Fürst Bismarck
• BC12 Manteuffel
• BC13 Steinmetz
• BC14 Arminius
• BC18 K Augusta
• BC19 Hansa
• BC20 Roon
• BC21 Yorck
• BC22 Victoria Louise
• BC23 Hertha
• BC24 Freya
• BC25 Vineta
• AC17 Henk
• AC19 Maass
• AC20 Maerker
• AC21 Ariadne
• AC22 Undine
• AC23 Meteor
• AC24 Comet
• AC25 Lorelei
• AC26 Greif
• CL44 Cöln ii
• CL45 Wiesbaden ii
• CL46 Dresden ii
• CL47 Magdeburg ii
• CL48 Leipzig ii
• CL49 Rostock ii
• CL50 Frauenlob ii
• CL57 Bremen
• CL58 Metz
• CL59 Kolmar
• CL60 Dortmund
• CL61 Duisburg
• CL62 Düsseldorf
• 20 x V170-class DD
• 30 x S49-class DD

Within one sea zone of Wilhelmshaven (AB 31):
Support Force
• BB18 Bayern
• BB19 Baden
• BB20 Sachsen
• BB21 Württemberg
• BB31 Prinz Georg
• BB32 Prinz Ferdinand
• BB33 K F Wilhelm
• BB34 Hermann von Salza
• BB35 Fritigern
• BB36 Brandenburg
• BB37 Weissenburg
• BB38 Wörth
• BB39 Spichern
• BB40 Friedrich III
• BB41 Wilhelm II
• BB42 Wilhelm der Grosse
• BB43 Karl der Grosse
• BB44 Barbarossa
• BB45 Pommern
• BB46 Wittelsbach
• BB47 Wettin
• AC01 Blücher
• AC08 Prinz Moritz
• AC09 Königin Luise
• AC10 S von Utrecht
• AC11 Prinz Leopold
• AC12 Stosch
• CL32 Graudenz '15
• CL33 Regensburg '17
• CL36 Wiesbaden
• CL37 Frankfurt
• CL38 Brummer
• CL39 Bremse
• CL40 Königsberg ii
• CL41 Karlsruhe ii
• CL42 Emden ii
• CL43 Nürnberg ii
• CL53 Potsdam
• CL54 Göttingen
• CL55 Freiburg
• CL56 Konstanz
• DD100 S113
• DD101 S114
• DD102 S115
• DD103 V116
• DD104 V117
• DD105 V118
• DD106 G119
• DD107 G120
• DD108 G121
• DD109 B122
• DD110 B123
• DD111 B124
• 36 x S49-class DD

Airships
At Cuxhaven (AA 35):
• L30   • L41   • L42   • L54
• L56   • L60   • L61

Submarines
Ten submarines may be set up in any eligible sea zones.

Allied Forces
At Scapa Flow (K 21):
Northern Patrol
• BC02 Inflexible
• BC03 Indefatigable
• BC04 New Zealand
• BC21 Intrepid
• AC01 Minotaur
• AC02 Shannon
• AC03 Defence
• 15 x Admiralty-class DD

Sea Zone I 25:
• BC01 Indomitable

Sea Zone H 27:
• BC02 Australia (RAN)

Sea Zone G 30:
• BC05 Invincible

At Rosyth (R 18):
Battle Cruiser Fleet
• BB23 Queen Elizabeth, Leader Beatty
• BB24 Warspite   • BB25 Valiant
• BB26 Barham   • BB27 Malaya
• BB96 King Henry V   • BC06 Lion
• BC07 Princess Royal   • BC08 Queen Mary
• BC09 Tiger   • BC10 Leopard
• BC16 Hood   • BC17 Rodney
• BC18 Howe   • BC19 Anson
• BC20 Sans Pareil   • BC22 Unicorn
• AC50 Surprise   • AC51 Seahorse
• AC52 Seringapatam   • AC53 Severn
• CL55 Danae   • CL56 Dragon
• CL57 Dauntless   • CL58 Delhi
• CL59 Dunedin   • CL63 Hawkins
• CL64 Cavendish   • 30 x W-class DD

At Cromarty (N 19):
• BB11 Conqueror   • BB12 Monarch
• BB13 Orion   • BB14 Thunderer
• BB15 King George V   • BB16 Centurion
• BB17 Audacious   • BB18 Ajax
• BB19 Iron Duke   • BB20 Marlborough
• BB21 Benbow   • BB22 Emperor of India
• BB28 Ramillies   • BB29 Resolution
• BB30 Revenge   • BB31 Royal Oak
• BB32 R Sovereign   • BB43 Renown
• BB44 Repulse   • BB45 Resistance
• BB46 Ocean   • BB47 Devastation
• BB48 Hero   • BB49 Irresistible
• BB50 Nemesis   • BB51 Retribution
• BB52 Powerful   • BB53 Terrible
• CL38 Centaur   • CL39 Concord
• CL40 Calypso   • CL41 Caradoc
• CL42 Cassandra   • CL43 Caledon
• CL44 Ceres   • CL45 Cardiff
• CL46 Curacoa   • CL47 Coventry
• CL48 Curlew   • CL50 Carlisle
• CL51 Calcutta   • CL52 Cairo
• CL53 Colombo   • CL54 Capetown
• CVS03 Riviera   • CVS04 Engadine
    • 1 x S.184 (S)   • 1 x S.184 (S)
• 12 x W-class DD   • 60 x Admiralty-class DD

Submarines
Four submarines may be set up in any eligible sea zones.

Special Rules
Minefields: The Central Powers player place six minefields adjacent to German coastal zones (from AB 30 to Y 35, inclusive, including the island of Helgoland, Zone Y 32, and the island of Scharhörn, Zone Z 33).

Coming Home: Every even-numbered turn, the Central Powers player may write down the location of one merchant ship in any sea zone on the northern edge of the map. The ship does not require a fleet marker and is given a Raid mission. If located by the Allied player, the ship is removed from play and the Allied player receives VPs, as shown below.

Twice per game, the Central Powers player may choose a liner as the merchant ship. A liner has a speed of 2. The Allied player receives 10 VPs for intercepting a liner; the Central Powers player receives 12 VPs if the liner enters a German port.

Ten times per game, the Central Powers player may choose a fast merchant as the merchant ship. A fast merchant has a speed of 1. The Allied player receives four VPs for intercepting a fast merchant; the Central Powers player receives six VPs if the fast merchant enters a German port.

On the remaining turns, the Central Powers player may choose a slow merchant as the merchant ship. A slow merchant has a speed of 1-slow. The Allied player receives three VPs for intercepting a slow merchant; the Central Powers player receives five VPs if the slow merchant enters a German port.

The Central Powers player is never required to enter a merchant ship; he or she may let the entire game pass without a merchant ship's entry. Merchant ships are moved as the Central Powers player pleases.

Victory Conditions
The player with the most VPs at the end of play wins.

OPERATIONAL SCENARIO SEVEN
Channel Dash
AUTUMN 1919

In any war with Germany, Britain's Royal Navy would first and foremost have to assure the safe passage of the British Expeditionary Force across the English Channel to Flanders. In the actual Great War, the Channel Fleet deployed pre-dreadnoughts to help secure the passage, and eventually the original Dreadnought herself. Had war come to Europe a few years later, the Channel Fleet would still have had plenty of older ships on which to draw.

Time Frame: 40 turns
Starting Weather: 2 (Mist)
Starting Turn: Central Powers player's choice

Central Powers Forces

Within ten sea zones of Wilhelmshaven (AB 31):
Scouting Force
- AC01 Blücher
- AC08 Prinz Moritz
- AC09 Königin Luise
- AC10 Simon von Utrecht
- AC11 Prinz Leopold
- AC12 Stosch
- AC15 Gefion, Leader Hipper
- AC16 Dorothea
- AC17 Henk
- AC18 Bevern
- AC19 Maass
- AC20 Maerker
- AC21 Ariadne
- AC22 Undine
- AC23 Meteor
- AC24 Comet
- AC25 Lorelei
- AC26 Greif
- 25 x V170-class DD

At or within one sea zone of zone AA27:
Raiding Force
- BB48 Jasmund, Leader Souchon
- BB49 Eckernförde
- BB50 Sedan
- BB51 Gravelotte
- BC05 Derfflinger
- BC06 Lützow
- BC07 Hindenburg
- BC08 Mackensen
- BC09 Prinz Eitel Friedrich
- BC10 Graf Spee
- BC11 Fürst Bismarck
- BC12 Manteuffel
- BC13 Steinmetz
- BC14 Arminius
- BC17 Schwerin
- BC18 K Augusta
- BC19 Hansa
- BC20 Roon
- BC21 Yorck
- BC22 Victoria Louise
- BC23 Hertha
- BC24 Freya
- BC25 Vineta
- CL38 Brummer
- CL39 Bremse
- CL44 Cöln ii
- CL45 Wiesbaden ii
- CL46 Dresden ii
- CL47 Magdeburg ii
- CL48 Leipzig ii
- CL49 Rostock ii
- CL50 Frauenlob ii
- CL57 Bremen
- CL58 Metz
- CL59 Kolmar
- CL60 Dortmund
- CL61 Duisburg
- CL62 Düsseldorf
- CL63 Thorn
- CL64 Memel
- 30 x S49-class DD

Within one sea zone of Wilhelmshaven (AB 31):
Support Force
- BB18 Bayern
- BB19 Baden
- BB20 Sachsen
- BB21 Württemberg
- BB31 Prinz Georg
- BB32 Prinz Ferdinand
- BB33 K F Wilhelm
- BB34 Hermann von Salza
- BB35 Fritigern
- BB36 Brandenburg
- BB37 Weissenburg
- BB38 Wörth
- BB39 Spichern
- BB40 Friedrich III
- BB41 Wilhelm II
- BB42 Wilhelm der Grosse
- BB43 Karl d Grosse
- BB44 Barbarossa
- BB45 Pommern
- BB46 Wittelsbach
- BB47 Wettin
- CL32 Graudenz '15
- CL33 Regensburg '17
- CL36 Wiesbaden
- CL37 Frankfurt
- CL40 Königsberg ii
- CL41 Karlsruhe ii
- CL42 Emden ii
- CL43 Nürnberg ii
- CL53 Potsdam
- CL54 Göttingen
- CL55 Freiburg
- CL56 Konstanz
- DD100 S113
- DD101 S114
- DD102 S115
- DD103 V116
- DD104 V117
- DD105 V118
- DD106 G119
- DD107 G120
- DD108 G121
- DD109 B122
- DD110 B123
- DD111 B124
- 36 x S49-class DD

Airships
At Cuxhaven (AA 35):
- L30
- L41
- L42
- L54
- L56
- L60
- L61

Submarines
Ten submarines may be set up in any eligible sea zones.

Allied Forces

At Sheerness (AE 22):
Channel Fleet
- BB01 Dreadnought
- BB02 Superb
- BB03 Temeraire
- BB04 Bellerophon
- BB05 Collingwood
- BB06 St. Vincent
- BB07 Vanguard
- BB08 Neptune
- BB09 Colossus
- BB10 Hercules
- BB93 Captain
- BB94 Elephant
- BB95 Atlas
- BB97 Nile
- BB98 Camperdown
- CL24 Cordelia '18
- CL25 Comus '18
- CL26 Caroline '18
- CL27 Carysfort '18
- CL28 Cleopatra '18
- CL29 Conquest '18
- CL30 Calliope '18
- CL31 Champion '18
- CL34 Canterbury '18
- CL35 Castor '18
- CL36 Cambrian '18
- CL37 Constance '18
- 40 x Admiralty-class DD

At Rosyth (R 18):
Battle Cruiser Fleet
- BB23 Queen Elizabeth, Leader Beatty
- BB24 Warspite
- BB25 Valiant
- BB26 Barham
- BB27 Malaya
- BB96 King Henry V
- BC06 Lion
- BC07 Princess Royal
- BC08 Queen Mary
- BC09 Tiger
- BC10 Leopard
- BC16 Hood

- BC17 Rodney
- BC19 Anson
- BC22 Unicorn
- AC51 Seahorse
- AC53 Severn
- CL56 Dragon
- CL58 Delhi
- CL63 Hawkins
- 30 x W-class DD

- BC18 Howe
- BC20 Sans Pareil
- AC50 Surprise
- AC52 Seringapatam
- CL55 Danae
- CL57 Dauntless
- CL59 Dunedin
- CL64 Cavendish

At Scapa Flow (K 21):
- BB11 Conqueror
- BB13 Orion
- BB15 King George V
- BB17 Audacious
- BB19 Iron Duke
- BB21 Benbow
- BB28 Ramillies
- BB30 Revenge
- BB32 R Sovereign
- BB44 Repulse
- BB46 Ocean
- BB48 Hero
- BB50 Nemesis
- BB52 Powerful
- CL38 Centaur
- CL40 Calypso
- CL42 Cassandra
- CL44 Ceres
- CL46 Curacoa
- CL48 Curlew
- CL51 Calcutta
- CL53 Colombo
- CVS03 Riviera
  - 1 x S.184 (S)
- 12 x W-class DD

- BB12 Monarch
- BB14 Thunderer
- BB16 Centurion
- BB18 Ajax
- BB20 Marlborough
- BB22 Emperor of India
- BB29 Resolution
- BB31 Royal Oak
- BB43 Renown
- BB45 Resistance
- BB47 Devastation
- BB49 Irresistible
- BB51 Retribution
- BB53 Terrible
- CL39 Concord
- CL41 Caradoc
- CL43 Caledon
- CL45 Cardiff
- CL47 Coventry
- CL50 Carlisle
- CL52 Cairo
- CL54 Capetown
- CVS04 Engadine
  - 1 x S.184 (S)
- 60 x Admiralty-class DD

Submarines
Four submarines may be set up in any eligible sea zones.

Special Rules
Minefields: The Central Powers player place six mine-fields adjacent to German coastal zones (from AB 30 to Y 35, inclusive, including the island of Helgoland, Zone Y 32, and the island of Scharhörn, Zone Z 33). The Allied player may place two minefields adjacent to any coastal zone of Britain.

Advance Scouts: Up to three airships (drawn randomly from available airships) may be placed within three zones of any Central Powers fleet. They have used one-third of their endurance.

Victory Conditions
The Central Powers player receives one VP for each bombardment hit from primary guns scored against Dover (AF 22), Dunkerque (AG 23) or any coastal zone adjacent to either port. The Central Powers player wins if he or she scores at least 20 more VPs than the Allied player. The Allied player wins if he or she scores more VPs than the Central Powers player. Any other result is a draw

OPERATIONAL SCENARIO EIGHT
Exit, Stage Left
AUTUMN 1919

During the actual Great War the High Seas Fleet never sent any of its cruisers into the North Atlantic to attack enemy commerce. Both the Germans and the British discussed this possibility, which could have brought on a fleet battle had the High Seas Fleet come out to escort the would-be raider past the British distant blockade. The German command finally decided not to risk the loss of any of its cruisers on such a mission, but the British didn't know that.

Time Frame: 70 turns
Starting Weather: 2 (Mist)
Starting Turn: Central Powers player's choice

Central Powers Forces
Within six sea zones of Wilhelmshaven (AB 31):
Scouting Force
- BB48 Jasmund
- BB50 Sedan
- BC05 Derfflinger
- BC06 Lützow, Leader Hipper
- BC07 Hindenbur
- BC09 Prz E Friedrich
- BC11 Fürst Bismarck
- BC13 Steinmetz
- BC17 Schwerin
- BC19 Hansa
- BC21 Yorck
- BC23 Hertha
- BC25 Vineta
- AC08 Prinz Moritz
- AC10 S von Utrecht
- AC12 Stosch
- AC16 Dorothea
- AC18 Bevern
- AC20 Maerker
- AC22 Undine
- AC24 Comet
- AC26 Greif
- CL39 Bremse

- BB49 Eckernförde
- BB51 Gravelotte

- BC08 Mackensen
- BC10 Graf Spee
- BC12 Manteuffel
- BC14 Arminius
- BC18 Kaiserin Augusta
- BC20 Roon
- BC22 Victoria Louise
- BC24 Freya
- AC01 Blücher
- AC09 Königin Luise
- AC11 Prinz Leopold
- AC15 Gefion
- AC17 Henk
- AC19 Maass
- AC21 Ariadne
- AC23 Meteor
- AC25 Lorelei
- CL38 Brummer
- CL44 Cöln ii

- CL45 Wiesbaden ii
- CL46 Dresden ii
- CL47 Magdeburg ii
- CL48 Leipzig ii
- CL49 Rostock ii
- CL50 Frauenlob ii
- CL57 Bremen
- CL58 Metz
- CL59 Kolmar
- CL60 Dortmund
- CL61 Duisburg
- CL62 Düsseldorf
- CL63 Thorn
- CL64 Memel
- 20 x V170-class DD
- 30 x S49-class DD
- 3 x collier (fast merchant)

Within one sea zone of Wilhelmshaven (AB 31):
Support Force
- BB18 Bayern
- BB19 Baden
- BB20 Sachsen
- BB21 Württemberg
- BB31 Prinz Georg
- BB32 Prinz Ferdinand
- BB33 K F Wilhelm
- BB34 Hermann von Salza
- BB35 Fritigern
- BB36 Brandenburg
- BB37 Weissenburg
- BB38 Wörth
- BB39 Spichern
- BB40 Friedrich III
- BB41 Wilhelm II
- BB42 Wilhelm der Grosse
- BB43 Karl der Grosse
- BB44 Barbarossa
- BB45 Pommern
- BB46 Wittelsbach
- BB47 Wettin
- CL32 Graudenz '15
- CL33 Regensburg '17
- CL36 Wiesbaden
- CL37 Frankfurt
- CL40 Königsberg ii
- CL41 Karlsruhe ii
- CL42 Emden ii
- CL43 Nürnberg ii
- CL53 Potsdam
- CL54 Göttingen
- CL55 Freiburg
- CL56 Konstanz
- DD100 S113
- DD101 S114
- DD102 S115
- DD103 V116
- DD104 V117
- DD105 V118
- DD106 G119
- DD107 G120
- DD108 G121
- DD109 B122
- DD110 B123
- DD111 B124
- 36 x S49-class DD

Airships
At Cuxhaven (AA 35):
- L30
- L41
- L42
- L54
- L56
- L60
- L61

Submarines
Ten submarines may be set up in any eligible sea zones.

Allied Forces
At Scapa Flow (K 21):
Northern Patrol
- BC02 Inflexible
- BC03 Indefatigable
- BC04 New Zealand
- BC21 Intrepid
- AC01 Minotaur
- AC02 Shannon
- AC03 Defence
- 15 x Admiralty-class DD

Sea Zone I 25:
- BC01 Indomitable

Sea Zone H 27:
- BC02 Australia (RAN)

Sea Zone G 30:
- BC05 Invincible

At Rosyth (R 18):
Battle Cruiser Fleet
- BB23 Queen Elizabeth, Leader Beatty
- BB24 Warspite
- BB25 Valiant
- BB26 Barham
- BB27 Malaya
- BB96 King Henry V
- BC06 Lion
- BC07 Princess Royal
- BC08 Queen Mary
- BC09 Tiger
- BC10 Leopard
- BC16 Hood
- BC17 Rodney
- BC18 Howe
- BC19 Anson
- BC20 Sans Pareil
- BC22 Unicorn
- AC50 Surprise
- AC51 Seahorse
- AC52 Seringapatam
- AC53 Severn
- CL55 Danae
- CL56 Dragon
- CL57 Dauntless
- CL58 Delhi
- CL59 Dunedin
- CL63 Hawkins
- CL64 Cavendish
- 30 x W-class DD

At Cromarty (N 19):
- BB11 Conqueror
- BB12 Monarch
- BB13 Orion
- BB14 Thunderer
- BB15 King George V
- BB16 Centurion
- BB17 Audacious
- BB18 Ajax
- BB19 Iron Duke
- BB20 Marlborough
- BB21 Benbow
- BB22 Emperor of India
- BB28 Ramillies
- BB29 Resolution
- BB30 Revenge
- BB31 Royal Oak
- BB32 R Sovereign
- BB43 Renown
- BB44 Repulse
- BB45 Resistance
- BB46 Ocean
- BB47 Devastation
- BB48 Hero
- BB49 Irresistible
- BB50 Nemesis
- BB51 Retribution
- BB52 Powerful
- BB53 Terrible
- CL38 Centaur
- CL39 Concord
- CL40 Calypso
- CL41 Caradoc
- CL42 Cassandra
- CL43 Caledon
- CL44 Ceres
- CL45 Cardiff
- CL46 Curacoa
- CL47 Coventry
- CL48 Curlew
- CL50 Carlisle
- CL51 Calcutta
- CL52 Cairo
- CL53 Colombo
- CL54 Capetown
- CVS03 Riviera
- CVS04 Engadine
  - 1 x S.184 (S)
  - 1 x S.184 (S)
- 12 x W-class DD
- 60 x Admiralty-class DD

Submarines

Four submarines may be set up in any eligible sea zones.

Special Rules

Minefields: The Central Powers player may place ten minefields adjacent to German coastal zones (from AB 30 to Y 35, inclusive, including the island of Helgoland, Zone Y 32, and the island of Scharhörn, Zone Z 33). The Allied player may place eight minefields adjacent to any coastal zone of Britain.

Straits of Dover: Central Powers ships may not enter zones AF 22 or AG 23 due to numerous minefields.

Advance Scouts: Up to three airships (drawn randomly from available airships) may be placed within three zones of any Central Powers fleet. Mark off one-third of their endurance.

Victory Conditions

The Central Powers player receives twice the VP value of any CL and collier that exits the map between zones A 01 and N 01 (inclusive) by the end of play (the CL and collier must exit together in order to claim the VP award; therefore the Central Powers player can only claim this VP award up to three times). The player with the most VPs at the end of play wins. The Central Powers player cannot win unless at least one CL/collier combination exits the map as specified above.

BATTLE SCENARIO ELEVEN
Iron Dogs and Splendid Cats
SUMMER 1919

The new battle cruisers of the Derfflinger class would have been the only ships with 12-inch (305mm) guns retained under the radical plan to rely only on the newest battleships and battle cruisers, though sentiment and the fallacy of sunk costs argued for the nearly-new König-class battleships as well. The tough "Iron Dog" and her sisters would still have been able to take enormous punishment, but not dish out as much as their even newer near-sisters.

Time Frame: Night
Weather Condition: 1 (Clear)

Central Powers Forces

• BC05 Derfflinger
• BC06 Lützow, Leader Hipper
• BC07 Hindenburg   • BC17 Schwerin
• CL38 Brummer   • CL39 Bremse
• 8 x V170-class DD

Allied Forces

• BC06 Lion   • BC07 Princess Royal
• BC08 Queen Mary   • BC22 Unicorn
• CL63 Hawkins   • CL64 Cavendish
• 10 x W-class DD

Special Rules

Setup: The Central Powers player sets up in the central shaded hexes per rule 7.23. The Allied player has the initiative and sets up three hexes away from any German ship.

Heart of Oak: No British ship may leave the tactical map.

Length of Battle: The game continues for four rounds, or until all ships of one side have been sunk or have exited the map per 7.33.

Victory Conditions

To win, a player must sink or cripple at least one enemy BC and score more VPs than his or her opponent; any other result is a draw.

BATTLE SCENARIO TWELVE
Cruiser Warfare
SUMMER 1919

As the battle cruiser and battleship types merged into a dual-purpose fast battleship, both German and British naval thinkers saw a need for a fast armored cruiser to fulfill the missions originally intended for battle cruisers. They would operate against enemy light cruisers supporting the destroyer flotillas, and also range ahead of the battle fleet to seek the enemy. Sometimes, they would find them.

Time Frame: Daylight
Weather Condition: 1 (Clear)

Central Powers Forces

• AC15 Gefion   • AC16 Dorothea
• AC17 Henk   • AC18 Bevern
• AC19 Maass   • AC20 Maerker
• CL63 Thorn   • CL64 Memel
• 12 x V170-class DD

Allied Forces
• BC09 Tiger   • BC10 Leopard
• AC50 Surprise   • AC51 Seahorse
• AC52 Seringapatam   • AC53 Severn
• 10 x W-class DD

Special Rules

Setup: The Central Powers player sets up in the central

shaded hexes per rule 7.23. The Allied player has the initiative and enters anywhere along the north-west edge of the Tactical Map.

Heart of Oak: No British ship may leave the tactical map.

Length of Battle: The game continues for four rounds, or until all ships of one side have been sunk or have exited the map per 7.33.

Victory Conditions
To win, a player must sink or cripple at least one enemy BC or two ACs and score more VPs than his or her opponent; any other result is a draw.

BATTLE SCENARIO THIRTEEN
Grand Fleets
SUMMER 1919

While the naval war — whether the actual conflict or that for which both sides planned — would consist of far more skirmishes, raids and escort missions than actual fleet battle, the dreadnoughts had been designed to fight each other in a massive showdown. Bringing the fleets together in a setting acceptable to both sides proved nearly impossible during the Great War, but that's far easier in a paper exercise.

Time Frame: Daylight
Weather Condition: 1 (Clear)

Central Powers Forces
Raiding Force
- BB48 Jasmund, Leader Souchon
- BB49 Eckernförde
- BB50 Sedan
- BB51 Gravelotte
- BC08 Mackensen
- BC09 Prz E Friedrich
- BC10 Graf Spee
- BC11 Fürst Bismarck
- BC12 Manteuffel
- BC13 Steinmetz
- BC14 Arminius
- BC18 K Augusta
- BC19 Hansa
- BC20 Roon
- BC21 Yorck
- BC22 Victoria Louise
- BC23 Hertha
- BC24 Freya
- BC25 Vineta
- AC21 Ariadne
- AC22 Undine
- AC23 Meteor
- AC24 Comet
- AC25 Lorelei
- AC26 Greif
- CL44 Cöln ii
- CL45 Wiesbaden ii
- CL46 Dresden ii
- CL47 Magdeburg ii
- CL48 Leipzig ii
- CL49 Rostock ii
- CL50 Frauenlob ii
- CL57 Bremen
- CL58 Metz
- CL59 Kolmar
- CL60 Dortmund
- CL61 Duisburg
- CL62 Düsseldorf
- 30 x S49-class DD

Support Force
- BB18 Bayern
- BB19 Baden
- BB20 Sachsen
- BB21 Württemberg
- BB31 Prinz Georg
- BB32 Prinz Ferdinand
- BB33 K F Wilhelm
- BB34 Hermann von Salza
- BB35 Fritigern
- BB36 Brandenburg
- BB37 Weissenburg
- BB38 Wörth
- BB39 Spichern
- BB40 Friedrich III
- BB41 Wilhelm II
- BB42 Wilhelm der Grosse
- BB43 Karl der Grosse
- BB44 Barbarossa
- BB45 Pommern
- BB46 Wittelsbach
- BB47 Wettin
- AC01 Blücher
- AC08 Prinz Moritz
- AC09 Königin Luise
- AC10 S von Utrecht
- AC11 Prinz Leopold
- AC12 Stosch
- CL32 Graudenz '15
- CL33 Regensburg '17
- CL36 Wiesbaden
- CL37 Frankfurt
- CL40 Königsberg ii
- CL41 Karlsruhe ii
- CL42 Emden ii
- CL43 Nürnberg ii
- CL53 Potsdam
- CL54 Göttingen
- CL55 Freiburg
- CL56 Konstanz
- DD100 S113
- DD101 S114
- DD102 S115
- DD103 V116
- DD104 V117
- DD105 V118
- DD106 G119
- DD107 G120
- DD108 G121
- DD109 B122
- DD110 B123
- DD111 B124
- 36 x S49-class DD

Allied Forces
Battle Cruiser Fleet
- BB23 Queen Elizabeth, Leader Beatty
- BB24 Warspite
- BB25 Valiant
- BB26 Barham
- BB27 Malaya
- BB96 King Henry V
- BC16 Hood
- BC17 Rodney
- BC18 Howe
- BC19 Anson
- BC20 Sans Pareil
- CL55 Danae
- CL56 Dragon
- CL57 Dauntless
- CL58 Delhi
- CL59 Dunedin
- 30 x W-class DD

Grand Fleet
- BB11 Conqueror
- BB12 Monarch
- BB13 Orion
- BB14 Thunderer
- BB15 King George V
- BB16 Centurion
- BB17 Audacious
- BB18 Ajax
- BB19 Iron Duke
- BB20 Marlborough
- BB21 Benbow
- BB22 Emperor of India
- BB28 Ramillies
- BB29 Resolution
- BB30 Revenge
- BB31 Royal Oak
- BB32 R Sovereign
- BB43 Renown
- BB44 Repulse
- BB45 Resistance
- BB46 Ocean
- BB47 Devastation
- BB48 Hero
- BB49 Irresistible

- BB50 Nemesis
- BB52 Powerful
- CL38 Centaur
- CL40 Calypso
- CL42 Cassandra
- CL44 Ceres
- CL46 Curacoa
- CL48 Curlew
- CL51 Calcutta
- CL53 Colombo
- 12 x W-class DD

- BB51 Retribution
- BB53 Terrible
- CL39 Concord
- CL41 Caradoc
- CL43 Caledon
- CL45 Cardiff
- CL47 Coventry
- CL50 Carlisle
- CL52 Cairo
- CL54 Capetown
- 70 x Admiralty-class DD

Special Rules

Set up and Initiative: The German Raiding Force sets up in the central shaded hexes, and the Support Force sets up anywhere along the south-west edge of the Tactical Map. The Battle Cruiser Fleet sets up in any hexes one hex away from the north-west edge of the Tactical Map, and the Grand Fleet sets up in any hexes along the north-east edge of the Tactical Map. The Allied player has the initiative for the first round.

Unmoving Map: The tactical map does not "move" in this scenario (see rule 7.33). Allied ships may only exit the northwest, north and northeast edges of the tactical map, and Central Powers ships may only exit the southeast or southwest edges of the tactical map. Ships that exit the map are removed from play immediately and the opposing player receives half their VP value (round fractions up).

Length of Battle: The game continues for eight rounds, or until all ships of one side have been sunk or have exited the map.

Victory Conditions

A player must sink or cripple at least four enemy BB or BC, and have more VPs at the end of play than his or her opponent, in order to win; any other result is a draw.

BATTLE SCENARIO FOURTEEN
Invincibles
Autumn 1919

The new German fast armored cruisers had not been built to face enemy battle cruisers, but they were larger than the British Inflexible class and could match their gunnery range, if not shell weight, with their excellent main battery. A North Sea meeting might even the score between German armored cruisers and British battle cruisers.

Time Frame: Daylight
Weather Condition: 1 (Clear)

Central Powers Forces
- AC15 Gefion
- AC16 Dorothea
- AC18 Bevern

Allied Forces
- BC02 Inflexible
- BC21 Intrepid

Special Rules

Setup: The Allied player sets up in the central shaded hexes per rule 7.23. The Central Powers player has the initiative and enters anywhere along the south-western edge of the Tactical Map.

Heart of Oak: No British ship may leave the tactical map.

Length of Battle: The game continues for four rounds, or until all ships of one side have been sunk or have exited the map per 7.33.

Victory Conditions

The player with the most VPs at the end of play wins. Neither player can win unless at least one enemy ship is crippled or sunk.

BATTLE SCENARIO FIFTEEN
Maze of the Minotaur
Autumn 1919

By 1919 the armored cruisers of the Minotaur class, Britain's last such ships built before the Great War, would only have been ten years old but still hopelessly outdated as modern fighting units. However, they would have been very useful on the Northern Patrol, where they would remain seaworthy and able to use all of their weapons in much rougher seas than could smaller cruisers. The problem, of course, would be that not every German ship encountered would be an unarmed freighter or liner.

Time Frame: Daylight
Weather Condition: 1 (Clear)

Central Powers Forces
- AC21 Ariadne
- AC25 Lorelei

Allied Forces
- AC01 Minotaur
- AC02 Shannon
- AC03 Defence
- 3 x Admiralty-class DD

Special Rules

Setup: The Allied player sets up in the central shaded hexes per rule 7.23. The Central Powers player has the initiative and sets up anywhere at least three hexes from the Allied ships.

Heart of Oak: No British ship may leave the tactical map.

Length of Battle: The game continues for four rounds, or until all ships of one side have been sunk or have exited the map per 7.33.

Victory Conditions
The Central Powers player wins if at the end of play all three British cruisers have been sunk and neither German cruiser has been sunk or crippled.

BATTLE SCENARIO SIXTEEN
Battle Cruiser Fleets
AUTUMN 1919

Both Britain and Germany built fast battleships, often still classing them as battle cruisers, and operated them separately from the van of the battle fleet. Each probed ahead of the main body, seeking the other. And when they clashed, it would result in a major surface battle all on its own.

Time Frame: Night
Weather Condition: 1 (Clear)

Central Powers Forces
Left Wing
• BB48 Jasmund, Leader Souchon
• BB49 Eckernförde • BB50 Sedan
• BB51 Gravelotte • BC18 Kaiserin Augusta
• BC19 Hansa • BC20 Roon
• BC21 Yorck • BC22 Victoria Louise
• BC23 Hertha • BC24 Freya
• BC25 Vineta • CL44 Cöln ii
• CL45 Wiesbaden ii • CL46 Dresden ii
• CL47 Magdeburg ii • CL48 Leipzig ii
• CL49 Rostock ii • CL50 Frauenlob ii
• CL57 Bremen • CL58 Metz
• CL59 Kolmar • 20 x V170-class DD

Right Wing
• BC08 Mackensen • BC09 Prinz Eitel Friedrich
• BC10 Graf Spee • BC11 Fürst Bismarck
• BC12 Manteuffel • BC13 Steinmetz
• BC14 Arminius • CL38 Brummer
• CL39 Bremse • CL60 Dortmund

• CL61 Duisburg • CL62 Düsseldorf
• CL63 Thorn • CL64 Memel
• 30 x S49-class DD

Allied Forces
Battle Cruiser Fleet, Right Wing
• BB23 Queen Elizabeth, Leader Beatty
• BB24 Warspite • BB25 Valiant
• BB26 Barham • BB27 Malaya
• BB96 King Henry V • BC16 Hood
• BC17 Rodney • BC18 Howe
• BC19 Anson • CL63 Hawkins
• CL64 Cavendish • 12 x W-class DD

Battle Cruiser Fleet, Left Wing
• BC06 Lion • BC07 Princess Royal
• BC08 Queen Mary • BC09 Tiger
• BC10 Leopard • BC20 Sans Pareil
• BC22 Unicorn • AC50 Surprise
• AC51 Seahorse • AC52 Seringapatam
• AC53 Severn • CL55 Danae
• CL56 Dragon • CL57 Dauntless
• CL58 Delhi • CL59 Dunedin
• 18 x W-class DD

Special Rules
Setup: The Allied Left Wing enters anywhere along the North-East edge of the Tactical Map; the Allied Right Wing enters anywhere along the West edge of the Tactical Map. The Central Powers Left Wing enters anywhere along the South-East edge of the Tactical Map; the Central Powers Right Wing enters anywhere along the East edge of the Tactical Map. Roll to determine initiative before the start of play.

Heart of Oak: No British ship may leave the tactical map.

Length of Battle: The game continues for six rounds, or until all ships of one side have been sunk or have exited the map per 7.33.

Victory Conditions
The Central Powers player wins if he or she scores 40 more VP than the Allied Player. The Allied Player wins if he or she scores more VP than the Central Powers player. Any other result is a draw. Neither player can win unless at least two enemy BB and/or BC have been sunk (not merely crippled) before the end of play.

Sea of Green

West of Britain, the Irish Sea divided Britain and Ireland, and provided access to the United Kingdom's largest commercial ports including the massive Port of Liverpool. German submarines infiltrated these waters starting in February 1915, when they were declared part of the war zone surrounding the British Isles. Three months later, the submarine U20 sank the liner *Lusitania* off the southern coast of Ireland, killing 1,198 of her passengers and crew.

While submarines preyed on merchant shipping in the Irish Sea, the High Seas Fleet did not deploy its surface ships as raiders in these waters. While the English Channel could be secured with minefields backed by destroyer flotillas, German ships still had the dangerous option of steaming around the north of the British Isles and descending on these vital commercial routes from the west. They had the range for these missions, but if damaged would have no neutral ports in which to take refuge and they still would have to make their way past British patrols in the North Sea.

Despite a great deal of discussion of the possibilities in both London and Berlin, the High Seas Fleet did not take this option. But we're not limited by such prudent thinking, and these scenarios open up a section of the JUTLAND game map rarely used in that game or in our HIGH SEAS FLEET book.

OPERATIONAL SCENARIO NINE
Western Approaches
SPRING 1919

Most of Britain's imports came through the ports facing the waters known as the "Western Approaches," chiefly Liverpool. The convoys heading to these ports faced danger from German submarines, but no German surface warships attempted to interfere during the course of the Great War. The possibility remained a serious concern for the Royal Navy.

Time Frame: 60 turns
Starting Weather: 1 (Clear)
Starting Turn: Allied player's choice

Central Powers Forces
At or within one zone of Sea Zone P 04:
Mark two fuel boxes off each ship.
- BC21 Yorck
- AC16 Dorothea
- AC21 Ariadne

Lifeboats take HMS *Audacious* crew members to RMS *Olympic*.

At or within one zone of Sea Zone P 13:
Mark two fuel boxes off each ship.
- BC20 Roon
- CL60 Dortmund
- CL61 Duisburg
- CL62 Düsseldorf

Submarines
Twelve submarines may be set up in any eligible sea zones.

Allied Forces
At Scapa Flow (K 21):
- BC06 Lion
- BC07 Princess Royal
- BC08 Queen Mary
- BC22 Unicorn
- BC09 Tiger
- BC10 Leopard
- AC01 Minotaur
- AC02 Shannon
- AC03 Defence
- CL24 Cordelia '18
- CL25 Comus '18
- CL26 Caroline '18
- CL27 Carysfort '18
- 16 x W-class DD

At Lough Swilly (R 10):
- CL11 Dublin
- 12 x Tribal-class DD

At Queenstown (AB 07):
- BB31 Utah (USN)
- BB36 Nevada (USN)
- BB37 Oklahma (USN)
- 16 x Admiralty-class DD

Sea Zone AQ 1:
Convoy
Mark two fuel boxes off each ship.
- B05 Commonwealth
- B06 Hindustan
- B09 Africa
- B10 Britannia
- CL22 Royalist
- CL23 Inconstant
- 18 x fast transport
- 24 x slow transport

Special Rules

Heart of Oak: No British ship may leave the tactical map during tactical combat.

Outdated Engines: The British B05 Commonwealth, B06 Hindustan, B09 Africa and B10 Britannia have a speed of one-slow.

Commerce Raiding: Central Powers fleets with raiding or intercept missions may search for enemy merchant ships on the Merchant Location Table. Sea zones have the following merchant densities: within three sea zones of any British port, 4; within six sea zones of any British port, 2. Subtract one from the die roll result if within the specified distance of a British major port; subtract an additional one from the die roll result if the port is Liverpool.

Victory Conditions

The Central Powers player receives two VPs for each merchant sunk on the MLT, four VPs for each slow transport sunk and eight VPs for each fast transport sunk. The Allied player receives two VPs for each slow transport and four VPs for each fast transport which enters Bristol or Liverpool before the end of play. The Central Powers player must score at least 30 VPs, and score more VPs than the Allied player, in order to win; any other result is an Allied victory. The Allied player cannot win if fewer than six transports enter a British port (in Britain or Ireland) before the end of play.

OPERATIONAL SCENARIO TEN
The Foggy Dew
SPRING 1919

Irish efforts to free the island of British occupation would draw interest, and support, from Germany. The Irish Republican Army needed arms, and the German proved willing to supply them. But first they would have to run them past the ever-watchful Royal Navy.

> **Time Frame:** 60 turns
> **Starting Weather:** 1 (Clear)
> **Starting Turn:** Allied player's choice

Central Powers Forces

At or within one zone of Sea Zone B 14:
Mark two fuel boxes off each ship.
- AC15 Gefion
- AC16 Dorothea
- AC21 Ariadne
- AC24 Comet
- CL60 Dortmund
- CL61 Duisburg
- CL62 Düsseldorf

Submarines
Twelve submarines may be set up in any eligible sea zones.

Allied Forces

At Scapa Flow (K 21):
- BC06 Lion
- BC07 Princess Royal
- BC08 Queen Mary
- BC22 Unicorn
- BC09 Tiger
- BC10 Leopard
- CL24 Cordelia '18
- CL25 Comus '18
- CL26 Caroline '18
- CL27 Carysfort '18
- 16 x W-class DD

At Lough Swilly (R 10):
- AC01 Minotaur
- AC02 Shannon
- AC03 Defence
- CL01 Loverpool
- CL02 Bristol
- CL11 Dublin
- CL14 Nottingham
- CL15 Lowestoft
- 12 x Tribal-class DD

At Queenstown (AB 07):
- AC04 Warrior
- AC05 Natal
- AC06 Achilles
- AC07 Cochrane
- AC08 Duke of Ednbrgh
- CL16 Aurora
- CL17 Arethusa
- CL18 Undaunted
- CL19 Galatea
- 16 x Admiralty-class DD

Special Rules

Heart of Oak: No British ship may leave the tactical map during tactical combat.

Arming the Irish: Before play begins, the Central Powers player may designate up to two ships as loaded with weapons. Each loaded ship has its secondary gunnery reduced by two as long as it remains loaded. The Central Powers player receives eight VPs for each ship which unloads in a coastal zone of Ireland before the end of play.

Commerce Raiding: Central Powers fleets with raiding or intercept missions may search for enemy merchant ships on the Merchant Location Table. Sea zones have the following merchant densities: within three sea zones of any British port, 4; within six sea zones of any British port, 2. Subtract one from the die roll result if within the specified distance of a British major port; subtract two from the die roll result if the port is Liverpool.

Victory Conditions

The Central Powers player receives two VPs for each secondary bombardment hit scored against port zones of Ireland, and one VP scored for each primary or secondary bombardment hit scored against zones adjacent to port zones of Ireland, and two VPs for each merchant sunk on the MLT, as well as any VPs scored for arming the Irish. The Central Powers player must score at least 20 VPs, and score more VPs than the Allied player, in order to win; any other result is an Allied victory.

BATTLE SCENARIO SEVENTEEN
Irish Sea
SPRING 1919

While the German raiders entering Irish waters would be among the High Seas Fleet's newest warships — which explains the fleet command's reluctance to approve such missions — those defending British interests would be among the Royal Navy's oldest vessels still in active service. That would create a mis-match should surface action result, but British sailors would not turn away from a fight in their home seas.

Time Frame: Daylight
Weather Condition: 1 (Clear)

Central Powers Forces
- AC15 Gefion
- AC16 Dorothea
- AC21 Ariadne
- AC24 Comet
- CL60 Dortmund
- CL61 Duisburg
- CL62 Düsseldorf

Allied Forces
First Cruiser Squadron
- AC01 Minotaur
- AC02 Shannon
- AC03 Defence
- CL01 Liverpool
- CL02 Bristol
- CL11 Dublin
- CL14 Nottingham
- CL15 Lowestoft
- 12 x Tribal-class DD

Second Cruiser Squadron
- AC04 Warrior
- AC05 Natal
- AC06 Achilles
- AC07 Cochrane
- AC08 Duke of Ednbrgh
- CL16 Aurora
- CL17 Arethusa
- CL18 Undaunted
- CL19 Galatea
- 16 x Admiralty-class DD

Special Rules
Setup: The Central Powers player sets up first in the central shaded hexes. The Allied First Cruiser Squadron enters anywhere along the north-west edge of the Tactical Map. The Allied Second Cruiser Squadron enters anywhere along the south-west edge of the Tactical Map. Roll for initiative at the start of play.

Heart of Oak: No British ship may leave the tactical map.

Length of Battle: The game continues for four rounds, or until all ships of one side have been sunk or have exited the map per 7.33.

Victory Conditions
The player with the most VPs at the end of play wins.

BATTLE SCENARIO EIGHTEEN
Sea Monster
SPRING 1919

British naval planners feared the prospect of a German battle cruiser escaping into the North Atlantic and attacking convoy traffic there, but did not fear it enough to detach modern warships from the Grand Fleet to defend the vulnerable merchants. Only in August 1918 did three American dreadnoughts go to Ireland to help defend against the threat; the convoys themselves had to be content with ancient pre-dreadnoughts at best.

Time Frame: Daylight
Weather Condition: 1 (Clear)

Central Powers Forces
- BC21 Yorck
- AC16 Dorothea
- AC21 Ariadne

Allied Forces
- B05 Commonwealth
- B06 Hindustan
- B09 Africa
- B10 Britannia
- CL22 Royalist
- CL23 Inconstant
- 18 x fast transport
- 24 x slow transport

Special Rules
Setup: The Allied player sets up first in the central shaded hexes. The Central Powers player has the initiative, and may enter from the north-east, east or south-east edge(s) of the Tactical Map in any combination he or she wishes.

Heart of Oak: No British ship may leave the tactical map.

Outdated Engines: The British B05 Commonwealth, B06 Hindustan, B09 Africa and B10 Britannia have a speed of one-slow.

Length of Battle: The game continues for four rounds, or until all ships of one side have been sunk or have exited the map per 7.33.

Victory Conditions
The Allied player receives three VPs for each transport that exits the north-east, east or south-east edge of the

Tactical Map, and loses three VPs for each transport that remains on the map at the end of play or exits the map via a different edge. The Central Powers player receives four VPs for each slow transport and eight VPs for each fast transport sunk. To win, a player must score at least 25 VPs, and have more VPs than his or her opponent; any other result is a draw.

BATTLE SCENARIO NINETEEN
Into the West
SPRING 1919

In the actual Great War, the U.S. Navy's Battleship Division Six arrived in Ireland in August 1918 with three modern battleships to provide a reaction force in case one or more German battle cruisers broke into the North Atlantic. While the American dreadnoughts had a great deal of firepower, they lacked the speed to chase down battle cruisers. Unless the battle cruisers sought a fight.

Time Frame: Daylight
Weather Condition: 1 (Clear)

Central Powers Forces
- BC20 Roon
- BC21 Yorck
- AC21 Ariadne
- CL61 Duisburg

Allied Forces
- BB31 Utah (USN)
- BB36 Nevada (USN)
- BB37 Oklahma (USN)
- 16 x Admiralty-class DD

Special Rules
Setup: The Allied player sets up first in the central shaded hexes. The Central Powers player has the initiative, and may enter from the north-west edge of the Tactical Map.

Heart of Oak: No British ship may leave the tactical map (note that the battleships are not British ships).

Length of Battle: The game continues for four rounds, or until all ships of one side have been sunk or have exited the map per 7.33.

Victory Conditions
The player with the most VPs at the end of play wins. Neither player can win unless at least one enemy battleship (BB) or battle cruiser (BC) has been sunk (not merely crippled).

BATTLE SCENARIO TWENTY
Bristol Fashion
SPRING 1919

German naval planners became concerned that their light cruisers had been manhandled by the larger, better-armed British light cruisers during the Battle of Jutland and other surface engagements. They sought larger cruisers of their own, with heavier gunnery, to take on the British.

Time Frame: Night
Weather Condition: 1 (Clear)

Central Powers Forces
- AC21 Ariadne
- AC24 Comet

Allied Forces
- AC04 Warrior
- AC05 Natal
- AC06 Achilles
- CL18 Undaunted
- CL19 Galatea

Special Rules
Setup: The Central Powers player sets up first in the central shaded hexes. The Allied player sets up second, anywhere outside the central shaded hexes. Roll for initiative at the start of play.

Heart of Oak: No British ship may leave the tactical map.

Length of Battle: The game continues for four rounds, or until all ships of one side have been sunk or have exited the map per 7.33.

Victory Conditions
The player with the most VPs at the end of play wins. Neither player can win unless at least one enemy ship has been sunk or crippled.

BATTLE SCENARIO TWENTY-ONE
The Nasty Old Leopard
SPRING 1919

A German battle cruiser breaking into the Atlantic would have to elude the Northern Patrol of elderly cruisers and armed merchantmen. But even if spotted, the battle cruiser would not be stopped by these ships. At best they could radio the position and heading of the would-be raider, and British battle cruisers could then take up the chase.

Time Frame: Daylight
Weather Condition: 1 (Clear)

Central Powers Forces
• BC21 Yorck   • AC16 Dorothea

Allied Forces
• BC09 Tiger   • BC10 Leopard

Special Rules
Setup: The Central Powers player sets up first in the central shaded hexes. The Allied player enters anywhere along the north-east edge of the Tactical Map. Roll for initiative at the start of play.
Heart of Oak: No British ship may leave the tactical map.

Length of Battle: The game continues for four rounds, or until all ships of one side have been sunk or have exited the map per 7.33.

Victory Conditions
The player with the most VPs at the end of play wins. Neither player can win unless at least one enemy ship has been sunk or crippled.

Four out of five Revenge-class battleships at sea.

British Battleships

In the autumn of 1912, First Lord of the Admiralty Winston Churchill and his staff began to craft the Royal Navy's 1913-1914 battleship construction program. The previous construction program had included four fast battleships of the Queen Elizabeth class, plus a fifth unit funded by the Federated Malay States; Parliament had already indicated that the new program would match the previous level of funding, but would not exceed it.

Churchill insisted that the program must include five capital ships, to maintain a superiority of 60 percent over the High Seas Fleet. That precluded his preferred option, to simply repeat the 1912 program of four *Queen Elizabeths*.

The Director of Naval Construction, Euston Tennyson d'Eyncourt, laid a variety of choices before the First Lord including repeats of the previous classes of dreadnought and battle cruiser (*Iron Duke* and *Tiger*) and improved versions of both designs featuring 15-inch guns rather than the 13.5-inch weapons of the older ships. Churchill desired two key qualities — battlecruiser-level speed and eight 15-inch guns — but D'Eyncourt could not deliver both of those in five ships and remain within the budgetary limits. If Churchill wanted five units, he could have slower ships, he could have fewer ships, or he could have weaker ships.

After railing against that hard reality for some weeks, in

November 1912 Churchill made his choice: five ships, each with eight 15-inch guns, reverting to the old fleet speed of 21 knots. D'Eyncourt began drafting the design based on an enlarged *Iron Duke* with four turrets rather than five. This ship would become the Revenge class, sometimes called the R-class or the Royal Sovereign class.

A year later, decisions had to be made for the next program. In January 1914 the Canadian government indicated that it would not, as had previously been discussed, fund three units of the Queen Elizabeth class. Recriminations flew over this "broken promise," but the crux of the disagreement came over Canadian insistence that Canadian dollars be spent in Canadian shipyards employing Canadian workers. In Britain, the politically powerful Vickers-Armstrong combine wished to see those dollars translated into sterling spent in Britain and exerted its influence to scuttle the deal rather than see battleship-building begin in the Dominions — even though Vickers owned the Canadian yards that would have received the orders.

To make up for the three "lost" ships, Churchill wrangled approval to accelerate the 1914 program, but not additional funding. He could therefore build four ships, and initially selected three repeat *Queen Elizabeths* and one repeat *Revenge*, later altering this to the reverse ratio, one repeat *Queen Elizabeth* and three repeat *Revenges*.

A *Revenge* supposedly could be built more quickly than a *Queen Elizabeth*, in theory, anyway — in practice the two types took about the same amount of time to complete (roughly 30 to 32 months) but none of the ships of either class had been commissioned at the time Churchill made his decision.

Contracts for the three Revenge-class ships were placed in May 1914, with two ships at private builders (*Repulse* at Palmers, Newcastle, and *Renown* at Fairfield, Glasgow) and one at a Royal Dockyard (*Resistance*, at Devonport). The one additional *Queen Elizabeth*, to be named *Agincourt*, was also placed at Devonport but a formal contract doesn't seem to have been issued for her. All four ships would have had improvements to their design, chiefly to their armor scheme, but otherwise have been nearly identical to those already under construction.

None of the ships of either class had been completed when Britain declared war on 4 August 1914. Three weeks later the Admiralty canceled the contract for *Resistance*, but only suspended those for *Repulse* and *Renown* — outright cancellation with a private firm would incur financial penalties, so the contracts were only "suspended." *Agincourt*'s delayed contract was simply not issued.

While construction of the three Revenge-class battleships halted (no keels had been laid or materials gathered), the orders for the dozen twin turrets for 15-inch Mark I rifles continued in force through either bureaucratic oversight or wartime profiteering. Ian Buxton in The Battleship Builders implies that the four turrets for *Resistance* were canceled and four new ones ordered later; Norman Friedman in British Battleships is clear that the turrets intended for *Resistance* were indeed manufactured (which, given the long lead times for these items, makes a great deal more sense).

Lord John Fisher took over as First Sea Lord in October 1914 for a tumultuous six-month hurricane of activity. During his brief reign, he found a legal loophole in the prohibition on new construction of capital ships, using the "suspended" contracts for *Repulse* and *Renown* to order a pair of battle cruisers under the same names. These two ships used six of the 12 turrets built by Vickers-Armstrong for the canceled/suspended Revenge-class ships. Four of the turrets went to the "large light cruisers" *Glorious* and *Courageous* (later to be re-used in the battleship *Vanguard*), and the remaining two were fitted in the monitors *Erebus* and *Terror*.

Fisher also took hold of the *Revenge* project, ordering a switch from mixed coal- and oil-firing boilers to uniform

A 15-inch twin turret under construction at Armstrong's Elswick Works.

oil power. That raised the ships' horsepower output from 31,000 to 40,000 and reduced their draft, theoretically raising their speed from 21 to 23 knots. On their trial runs none topped 21.9 knots, even though all five exceeded 40,000 horsepower. When Britain began to suffer oil shortages in 1917 the Revenge and Queen Elizabeth classes had restrictions on their use due to lack of fuel, while the coal-burning battleships continued to operate unimpeded.

The Revenge class met none of its requirements; ordered to save money, *Revenge* herself actually cost only slightly less than *Queen Elizabeth* (£2,556,368 for *Revenge* compared to £2,633,103 for *Queen Elizabeth*, or 97 percent). They proved cramped, slow and nearly impossible to modernize, with their main battery of eight excellent 15-inch Mark I naval rifles about their only redeeming feature. The Royal Navy would have been much better off retaining the battle cruiser *Tiger* during the 1930s naval reductions rather than one of these ships.

Repulse and *Renown*, completed as battle cruisers, became known as "Refit" and "Repair" in the fleet due to their myriad technical problems, and as built they were essentially unarmored: the largest and fastest capital ships in the world at the time, they were in essence a pair of very swift gunnery targets. Near-total reconstruction during the

1930s improved *Renown*, but neither proved to be a very good fighting ship.

While Churchill might have been better off building four more *Queen Elizabeths* instead, despite Royal Navy propaganda that class had its own flaws and none of them ever met their supposed top speed of 24 knots. These were not battleships able to catch battle cruisers, but simply very-well-armed dreadnoughts somewhat faster than other battleships. For the same price, Churchill could have had six more sister ships of the battle cruiser *Tiger*, which probably would have been a better investment, but then these ships wouldn't have been "new."

With the resignations of both Fisher and Churchill after the Dardanelles disaster in May 1915, the Admiralty began to look at new battleships again. Sir John Jellicoe, commander of the Grand Fleet, wanted more new battleships armed with 15-inch guns, as many as could be built as quickly as possible.

The new First Sea Lord, Admiral Sir Henry Jackson, placed battleships back on the table and in November 1915 the Treasury approved the expenditure for new ships despite growing financial distress. While the money had been made available for ships, it could not be stretched to cover new docks as well and so Jackson insisted that the new ship could not be longer than *Queen Elizabeth*.

Despite the flaws, British naval architects hit on a very fine design with the Queen Elizabeth class, a good combination of speed, firepower and protection — and also expense. *Iron Duke*, lead ship of the previous class, had cost £1.93 million while a new *Queen Elizabeth* was estimated to come in at nearly £3 million.

The size and budgetary restrictions also limited the main armament to that of *Queen Elizabeth*: eight 15-inch Mark I rifles, in four double turrets. Most of the designs submitted simply repeated the characteristics of *Queen Elizabeth*, with less speed. The Royal Navy already had such a ship in the unsatisfactory Revenge class; if Jackson had to accept a slower ship, he wanted one with stronger armament or superior protection, preferably both.

To achieve that, Jackson suggested moving to a triple turret for the 15-inch guns; a ship with two triple turrets and one double turret would have the same firepower as *Queen Elizabeth* but could be shorter, lighter and less costly. One with two triple turrets and two double turrets could have 25 percent more heavy guns on the same length, though it would likely displace more. D'Eyncourt, the Director of Naval Construction, argued against the triple turret on technical grounds, and Jackson relented on the size limit, agreeing to entertain proposals for a much larger ship that became the design for the battle cruiser *Hood*.

All of the proposals went to Jellicoe for comment, who now reversed his earlier positions. Where he had been willing to accept a 22-knot ship, he now wanted well-protected ships with at least 15-inch guns, fast enough to catch German battle cruisers. The tin-clad battle cruisers like *Glorious* or *Repulse* would be shredded by a German battle cruiser. And he now wanted guns larger than the 15-inch Mark I, having apparently heard of testing under way on the new 18-inch Mark I, an enlarged version of the 15-inch weapon.

To satisfy those expectations, the constructors continually modified the *Hood* design to improve speed and most of all protection in light of the experience of Jutland, or more correctly, inaccurate impressions of the experience of Jutland — British battle cruisers had been destroyed thanks to inadequate flash protection, not thin magazine armor. In May 1918, with Jellicoe now serving as First Sea Lord, d'Eyncourt tasked one of his assistants with studies of the triple 15-inch turret requested by Sir Henry Jackson — in August 1917 the accountants assigned to the *Hood* project had already suggested a switch to three triple turrets in place of the four twins as a cost-saving measure.

Design studies found that the barbette (the underlying armored "tower" supporting the gun turret) for the new triple turret would be five feet wider than the standard double turret's barbette. That would require a broader ship. A ship the size of *Hood* could be built with four triple turrets, at the price of cutting her speed from 32 knots to 27 knots. Alternatively, the triple turrets could be replaced with twin turrets mounting the "15-inch B" gun, the cover name for the 18-inch Mark I.

The 18-inch Mark I aboard the battle cruiser *Furious*.

Revenge-class *Royal Oak* at Malta.

After the end of the Great War, pressure to adopt the 18-inch gun mounted as the Americans provided information on their new battleships mounting 16-inch guns and word came that new Japanese ships would carry 16-inch guns as well. A new 18-inch gun, longer and more powerful than the Mark I, had undergone testing and was referred to as the 16-inch 50-caliber. Britain actually had no 16-inch guns under development at the time, but the Admiralty wished to remain a step ahead of its potential rivals in any case and did not wish to merely match their gunnery caliber.

In place of the *Hood*-derived designs, the constructors now began work on a series of proposals fitted with three triple turrets with the new-model 18-inch guns that eventually became the N-series designs. *Hood* herself would be completed, but her three sisters were cancelled as the Admiralty decided not to compound the decision to build a flawed ship by completing further units to the same design.

This book includes the three canceled Revenge-class battleships, as they were intended to be built. And there are two of the designs for new battleships.

First is the ten-gun version of *Queen Elizabeth* with two triple and two twin turrets, as initially requested by Sir Henry Jackson. She's slower than *Queen Elizabeth*, though as Jellicoe complained after Jutland the class could not make their designed speed anyway (and may not deserve their speed rating in Great War at Sea games), and the "fast wing" of the battle fleet turned out to be mostly a myth. The new ship — here called the Ocean class — is a powerful warship, with heavy firepower and good protection. Per Jellicoe's initial demand, she only makes 22 knots which is good for speed 1 in a Great War at Sea game.

The *Hood*-derived battleship with 18-inch guns is called the Nemesis class here (neither of these designs progressed far enough to be assigned construction contracts, let alone actual names — all eight of these ships carry traditional British capital ship names). She's a huge ship with enormous firepower and good protection, but as naval architects around the globe discovered it is very difficult to keep a ship's protection at a scale capable of repelling the fire of its own guns once massive weapons like the 18-inch Mark I have been fitted. For our version, we've given her better protection at the cost of horsepower, lowering her speed from the projected 27 knots to something closer to the 22-knot target of the Ocean class.

German Battleship Designs

In February 1916, Grand Admiral Alfred von Tirpitz established a new committee to study designs for future capital ships for the High Seas Fleet. They would determine the future look of the High Seas Fleet in light of wartime experience.

Germany had four new battleships under construction at the time, with *Baden* and *Bayern* nearing commissioning and their sisters *Sachsen* and *Württemberg* some months behind them. No other dreadnoughts had been laid down since the outbreak of the war, and new construction appeared unlikely until peace returned. But when peace did come, Tirpitz wanted to be ready for the true battle to commence: the battle over his service's funding.

Admiral Henning von Holtzendorff, Admiralty chief of staff, produced a memorandum in November 1915 pointing out the lower rate of fire of the 15-inch (380mm) guns carried by the Bayern class, compared to the 12-inch (305mm) guns of the preceding König class. Perhaps the new classes of battleship and battle cruiser ("large fighting ships" in German vernacular) should revert to the smaller guns and carry more of them, in triple or quadruple turrets.

An early proposal for the Bayern class would have fitted them with triple turrets bearing 13.8-inch (350mm) guns, a weapon retained for the Mackensen class battle cruisers but replaced in the battleship with dual turrets carrying the larger gun. German engineers visited the Austrian battleship *Viribus Unitis*, which carried triple turrets for her 12-inch guns, and came away unimpressed. The turret design required overly large openings in the armored deck, they argued, and a single hit or mechanical fault could render three guns inoperable rather than just two.

Admiral Georg von Müller, the head of Tirpitz's committee, raised an uncomfortable issue, what became known as the Typenfrage, the "Type Question." Germany had to date built both Linienschiffe ("ships of the line," or battleships) and Grosser Kreuzer ("Large Cruisers," used to designate what other nations termed protected cruisers, armored cruisers and battle cruisers). The most recent designs for battleships and battle cruisers had already begun to converge, with the most recently designed battle cruisers having cruiser speeds yet the protection and armament to stand in the line of battle with the dreadnoughts. This raised a potent political issue, as Tirpitz had secured separate funding lines for battleships and cruisers in Germany's Naval Laws and did not wish to upset this procedure.

Incomplete ships at Hamburg, probably 1920. From left, battle cruiser *Prinz Eitel Friedrich*, battleship *Württemberg* and Greek battleship *Salamis*.

That became less of a problem when Tirpitz was forcibly retired in March, allowing Müller to propose merging the two types into a single ship design, the Linienschiffs-kreuzer. This battleship-cruiser would have the speed of a battle cruiser, the protection of a battleship, the range to serve on overseas stations and a main armament capable of delivering "drumfire" — a term borrowed from then-current Army artillery practice, what later generations of naval thinkers would call "saturation fire."

For the first proposals it would study, the committee requested a fast-battleship version of the most recent German battleship, the *Bayern* design. The Construction Bureau duly handed over six design sketches on 19 April 1916: three for battleships, and three for battle cruisers. These went not only to the committee, but following normal practice to Kaiser Wilhelm II as well.

The new Navy chief, Eduard von Capelle, noted when forwarding the sketches that new developments had rendered earlier battleships obsolete. The High Seas Fleet needed to prepare for battles fought at a great distance from home bases and at long range, requiring ships with high speed and heavy guns. Toward that end, he suggested that it might become advisable to retire two of the High Seas Fleet's battleship squadrons — not only the pre-dreadnoughts of the Deutschland class, but the early dreadnoughts of the Nassau and Helgoland classes as well.

By that note, Capelle argued for a massive increase in battleship construction, since not only the pre-dreadnoughts but eight supposedly first-line dreadnoughts needed immediate replacement. The Kaiser remained non-committal, not throwing his weight behind Capelle's desire for many more dreadnoughts but not firing him for his effrontery, either.

The committee began its study, therefore, with at least a glimmer of hope that the ship it approved might actually be built. The three battleship designs, designated L1, L2 and L3 (for "Linienschiff"), all drew heavily on *Bayern* for their armor design and internal arrangements.

The hull was stretched, going from 183 meters long for *Sachsen* (the longest of the Bayern class) to 220 meters for L1 and L2 and 230 meters for L3. Each design differed in details, some of them significant. All three had a "mixed" power plant, with both coal- and oil-fired boilers.

L1 would be the simple "fast *Bayern*," with the same armor and mostly the same internal arrangements, adding another boiler room and six additional boilers, raising power output from 55,000 horsepower in *Württemberg* (the most powerful and fastest of the Bayern class) to 65,000 horsepower, and speed from 22.5 knots to 26 knots (with the longer, finer hull form contributing to this increase as well). The new ship displaced 38,500 tons at maximum load, compared to 32,500 for *Sachsen*.

L3 also had 18 boilers, but had larger oil-fired boilers than L1, producing 95,000 horsepower (this must be a misprint; the improved-Mackensen class battle cruisers made 100,000 horsepower with an enormously larger power plant). Whatever her output, it was enough to drive the ship at 26 knots, the same as L1, on a displacement 4,500 tons heavier.

The extra weight went to additional armor protection: for the first time, a German dreadnought added a thick armored deck in acknowledgement of the increased ranges at which future battles would be fought (thus bringing incoming enemy shells in at a higher angle) and added much thicker armor over her casemate, considered a potentially vulnerable area. Both designs carried the same armament as the Bayern class: eight 15-inch guns in four double turrets, sixteen 5.9-inch (150mm) guns in casemates, and five torpedo tubes with twenty torpedoes.

L2 started with the same hull as L1, but reduced the number of boilers to 15 from 18 and added a fifth turret for two 15-inch guns. This would be fitted in "C" position, stacked over the two aft turrets on a towering barbette. The design sketch claimed no displacement increase with the swap of boilers for barbette, which the commit

A König-class battleship, mid-war.

tee found questionable, which also brought the designed speed of 25 knots into doubt as well. And they wondered about stability issues brought on by that impossibly tall armored additional armored turret mount.

This book includes design L2 as the Kaiser Friedrich III class, and L3 as the Jasmund class. The Kaiser Friedrich III class are named for German emperors, and all are names used for early German pre-dreadnoughts. The Jasmund class ships are named for battles won by Germany or Prussia (or, in the case of Jasmund, stalemates claimed as victories).

None of these designs would be approved before the Battle of Jutland intervened, bringing a re-assessment of prevailing assumptions. Though German propagandists declared victory in the Battle of Jutland — known as the Battle of the Skaggerak in Germany — the High Seas Fleet's evaluations of the action and their ships shook the German admirals' confidence. In particular, the fast super-dreadnoughts of the Queen Elizabeth class made an enormous impression.

The High Seas Fleet's staff, writing in the name of fleet commander Reinhard Scheer, issued a memorandum pointing to three key factors that must be considered in the construction of new capital ships: heavier-caliber main guns, higher speed, and an emphasis on fast battleships rather than battlecruisers.

Scheer's staff did not endorse the concept of a "Unitary Warship" filling the role of both battleship and battle cruiser. As long as the British kept building battle cruisers, the Germans would need to do the same to support their scouting forces. But while the admirals and staff officers assigned to desks in Berlin studied the tactical reports and made their recommendations accordingly, the sea officers formed an economic argument.

The sheer size of the enemy's Grand Fleet, Scheer's staff wrote, made it unlikely that Germany could ever match the British ship-for-ship. And as long as the British held an advantage in fleet speed, they would be able to dictate the time and place of future fleet battles against the smaller German fleet, a recipe for disaster.

Therefore, the new capital ships should be individually superior to their British opponents: as fast as a battle cruiser, with protection at least sufficient against the 15-inch (380mm) guns of the newest British battleships, and a main armament heavier than the British 15-inch Mark I — the proposed 420mm (16.5-inch) SK L/45 gun, just entering the design stage at Krupp.

While the fleet staff did not dismiss battle cruisers, it pointed out that the next eight battle cruisers, including *Hindenburg* then fitting out at Wilhelmshaven's Imperial Dockyard, had already fallen behind the curve in terms of speed, protection, armament or all three. Therefore they felt it imperative to lay down a class of at least four new fast battleships armed with 420mm guns to redress the imbalance with the Grand Fleet.

The unrealistic nature of the demand bordered on the insane. *Hindenburg*'s sister ship *Derfflinger*, the fleet's "Iron Dog," had taken 29 months to go from keel-laying to commissioning. At the time of the fleet staff's Denkschrift the new battle cruiser had been under construction for 35 months already, and would not commission for another eight months — 43 total, or almost half again as long as *Derfflinger*. German shipyards simply did not have the labor to construct new capital ships while simultaneously building vast numbers of submarines and undertaking the necessary repair and refit work engendered by wartime action.

If the Imperial Dockyard could not complete a 26,000-ton battle cruiser in a reasonable length of time, it had no hope of building a 42,000-ton battleship in time to influence the outcome of the war. Even so, design work went forward on both the ship and the 420mm guns she would carry.

The Barbarossa class included with this book is the design variant known as L20e, presented to the Admiralty in August 1917. She was a huge ship, 235 meters long and displacing 42,000 tons (Germany's last completed battleship, *Baden*, displaced 28,000 tons on a 183-meter length). She would have belt and barbette armor of 350mm (just under 14 inches), the same as *Baden*, but thicker protection for her decks and less below the waterline.

Powering the ship would be 22 boilers, six fired by oil and the remainder by coal, with the coal-fired boilers having an auxiliary oil spray system to help the fuel burn hotter; the exhaust of all 22 boilers was trunked into a single gigantic funnel. Those boilers would provide steam to four turbines driving four shafts, an arrangement expected to produce just under 100,000 horsepower, nearly doubling *Baden*'s output of 55,000 horsepower. That would give the ship a designed speed of 23.5 knots and thereby yield an edge to *Queen Elizabeth*'s supposed 24 knots. Despite the experience of Jutland, the Germans do not seem to have been aware that these ships never met their designed speed — their new ship would have matched the British super-dreadnought or been very slightly faster.

Main armament would be eight 420mm rifles, in four twin turrets laid out almost exactly as those for the Ersatz Yorck class battle cruisers' 380mm guns with a large space between the two aft turrets, known in German parlance as C and D, because of the huge turbine room underneath them. Skoda had already designed and tested a 420mm naval gun, but the High Seas Fleet's intricate relationship with Krupp mandated a new design rather than a less-profitable license arrangement. The new gun would not be approved until September 1918. No prototypes of the big gun were ever built.

Secondary armament would be a dozen 150mm (5.9-inch) guns in an armored casemate, an arrangement going back to pre-dreadnought days. Eight heavy anti-aircraft guns, either 88mm or 105mm weapons, occupied single mounts on the deck. Three torpedo tubes would be carried as well, with an underwater tube at the bow and an above-water tube on either side, each tube having three torpedoes.

Though the architects had drafted an impressive warship, Scheer and his staffers were not impressed. The battleship was much too slow, and they wanted a ship that could make at least 30, preferably 32, knots. That required a

Battleship *Bayern* in British captivity.

Battleship *Bayern* on high-speed trials.

much bigger ship, to house the larger power plant and protect it with adequate armor. Subsequent schemes reduced the main armament to six guns to obtain higher speed, but these ships had even less chance of being built than the L20e design. Those ships had even less chance of being built than this ship. But Kaiser Wilhlem II gave his blessing: he did not care what form of battleship the committee chose, as long as one of them was named *Pommern* to honor the pre-dreadnought lost with all hands at Jutland.

This book includes the full class of four ships sought by the High Seas Fleet. They are well-protected with an impressive heavy armament, but are out-gunned by the new British battleship design with 18-inch guns under discussion in London at the same time. Scheer's insistence on high speed matches that of his counterpart Sir John Jellicoe, though unlike Scheer the British admiral indicated acceptance of a slower battleship as long as it carried 15-inch guns and could be brought into service as quickly as possible.

Both Scheer and Jellicoe overlooked an essential reality: each of them commanded a fleet including large numbers of ships armed with 11-inch, 12-inch and 13.5-inch guns, designed for a fleet speed of 21 knots maximum (and in the case of the oldest German dreadnoughts, even less than that). Unless Scheer wanted to steam out for battle with just the four new battleships, he would always be at a disadvantage in terms of numbers, speed and main armament.

German Battle Cruisers

Like naval architects in other nations, German warship designers shied away from superfiring turret arrangements, fearing that the blast effects from the upper turret would injure or even kill the crew of the lower battery. The United States Navy fitted superfiring turrets on its first dreadnoughts, the South Carolina class, without any damage to gun crews.

In Germany, retired Grand Admiral Hans von Koester, the newly elected president of the German Fleet Association (the politically powerful civilian booster club for naval expansion), pushed for adoption of what he called "the USN Pattern" — all gun turrets along a battleship's centerline, with super-firing pairs fore and aft. Koester had joined the Prussian Navy in 1859 and despite his age, Koester — a former naval architect himself — rejected the inherent conservatism of German warship design. While Germany had built two classes of dreadnoughts, they were technically much less advanced than those of the Royal Navy, not only in their turret layout but also their old-style reciprocating engines.

Despite testing at Krupp's proving ground that showed no excess pressure in the lower turret, the Germans moved slowly to adopt Koester's proposed arrangement, trying it out initially in the battle cruiser *Moltke*. Gun crews showed no ill effects, and German ships adopted the USN Pattern starting with the König-class dreadnoughts and Derfflinger-class battle cruisers.

Both the admirals and the architects realized that they had developed an extremely fine design with *Derfflinger*, ordered in 1911 and commissioned in 1914. She followed the USN Pattern, with two turrets forward and two aft. The two aft turrets had somewhat more separation between them, thanks to the larger turbine room below. *Derfflinger* combined speed, protection and firepower and the Germans repeated her design for the battle cruisers ordered under the 1912 (*Lützow*) and 1913 (*Hindenburg*) fiscal year programs.

Seeking heavier armament, but still enamored of the *Derfflinger* design, the Navy enlarged her and increased the main armament to 350mm (13.8-inch) for the battle cruiser ordered under the 1914 authorization (*Mackensen*) and ordered three more under the Wartime Construction Program. Another trio were ordered in April 1915 using additional special wartime funding made available to replace armored cruisers lost in action (*Scharnhorst*, *Gneisenau* and *Blücher*); these latter vessels had their

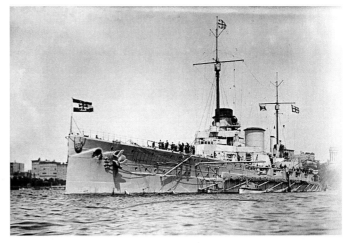

Battle cruiser *Moltke* visits New York, 1912.

main armament increased to 380mm (15-inch) guns but were otherwise very similar to *Mackensen* other than the noticeable difference of a huge single funnel.

Thus when the special committee convened by Alfred von Tirpitz to study new major warship construction for the High Seas Fleet met in the spring of 1916, Germany already had eight battle cruisers under construction or ordered. The committee spent a great deal of discussion on the Typenfrage, the question of whether the Navy should build both battleships and battle cruisers, or simply one class of fast battleship that could fill both roles.

So while the committee looked at fast battleship designs, it also continued to solicit sketches of new battle cruisers, "great cruisers" in German parlance. The Construction Department presented three new designs on 19 April 1916, adding a fourth a week later.

Like the Mackensen class, the new designs drew heavily from *Derfflinger*, adding another boiler room and slightly more length than *Mackensen*. All of the proposed ships carried a main armament of eight 15-inch guns in four turrets and sixteen 150mm (5.9-inch) guns in a casemate battery, plus eight 88mm anti-aircraft guns and five torpedo tubes.

All three designs also had an identical armor scheme to *Mackensen*. The differences lay in the power plants, and the changes to the hull that had to be made to accommodate them. GK1 had 32 boilers, producing 110,000 horsepower for 27 knots; GK2 had 36 boilers, producing 120,000 horsepower for 27.25 knots. GK3 also had 36 boilers, but produced only 115,000 horsepower for 27 knots.

Battle cruiser *Lützow* on speed trials.

That gave a slight increase in speed over the three improved Mackensens, which produced 100,000 horsepower from 32 boilers and was expected to make 28.75 knots; *Mackensen* herself made 90,000 horsepower for 27 knots.

Despite the incremental improvements in exchange for added costs and production delays, the committee liked the new proposals and recommended replacing the design for the three improved Mackensens with a new one. That decision owed more to naval politics than military necessity. A British submarine sank the elderly armored cruiser *Prinz Adalbert* in October 1915, opening a potential funding line for her replacement. But Kaiser Wilhelm warned his new Navy State Secretary (the Navy's political chief) Eduard von Capelle that the soaring costs of the new "great cruisers" could make approval difficult even during wartime — *Mackensen* had been projected to cost 66 million gold marks, compared to 58 million for *Hindenburg* ordered in the previous fiscal year. Whatever shipbuilding resources could be made available would have to go to expansion of the submarine force.

With approval for new ships in doubt — if even the Kaiser balked at the cost, the civilian leadership could not be counted on for support — Capelle and the admirals reasoned that the three new great cruisers for which they currently had approval might be the last until after the war ended and perhaps for some time afterward. In that case, it would be best to build those three ships to the most recent design available.

Work began in the summer of 1916, with one great cruiser order placed at each of three private shipyards: A.G. Vulkan in Hamburg, Krupp's Germaniawerft yard in Kiel and the Blohm & Voss yard in Hamburg that built most of Germany's great cruisers. Construction proceeded slowly, and unlike the Mackensen class work never formally stopped before the war ended though it appears that very little progress was made. Design work had not been completed when building began, though since the ship was so similar to *Mackensen* this probably would not have been a problem until the ship was far more advanced.

All three ships appeared in our JUTLAND game in their improved-*Mackensen* guise, as originally intended by the German Admiralty: the same hull as *Mackensen*, with bigger guns but no other appreciable differences. In this book they appear as the Admiralty also intended, four additional great cruisers built to the new design; in game terms there's not a lot of difference beyond the larger hull (the increase in ship speed isn't enough to affect game speed).

The Battle of Jutland, or Skaggerak, caused the German Admiralty to re-think its design principles for battle cruisers. The battle's results — or at least the German understanding of the battle's results — seemed to re-open the Typenfrage, the question of whether the Navy should build both battleships and battle cruisers, or simply one class of fast battleship that could fill both roles.

Spurred by the staff of the High Seas Fleet, the Admiralty decided to continue building battle cruisers, more for political than military reasons (under the German Naval Laws, battleships and cruisers came under separate funding lines). The new post-Jutland battle cruiser type would need to be at least as well-protected as those already under construction, and extraordinarily fast. The German great cruisers at Jutland had been at a seeming speed disadvantage compared to British fast battleships, let alone battle cruisers. The new ships needed to make at least 32 knots, and also had to carry the same 420mm (16.5-inch) main gun as the new post-Jutland battleships to assure superiority over British ships armed with 15-inch guns.

While the designers went with a larger proportion of oil-fired boilers than in any previous ships, they still relied on coal for the majority of the ship's power even though oil-fired boilers could provide more output. Their British had already built purely oil-fired battleships, but backed away with their Royal Sovereign class for strategic reasons, as high-grade coal could be mined in the British Isles but oil had not yet been discovered there. Germany faced a very similar situation, with even less access to petroleum, but her naval architects valued coal bunkers as an addition to a ship's protection scheme.

Three new great cruisers had been authorized in the late summer of 1916 and contracts placed in three private shipyards. By January only one keel had been laid and a small amount of work done on the other two. Vice Admiral Georg Hebbinghaus suggested that these authorizations be used with a new design, likely hoping to build his proposed fast armored cruiser on those slipways. His superiors had a bigger goal in mind — a much larger great cruiser armed with 420mm guns. Through a naval aide, the Kaiser indicated that "this did not disturb him in any way."

With German shipyards overwhelmed by repair work on existing ships and orders for new submarines and torpedo boats (destroyers), the new ship had little chance of being built even using the contracts already placed. Design work proceeded slowly, classed as a paper study rather than an active project, with sketches delivered in late February and early March 1918.

The two alternative designs, designated GK4542 and GK4541 (GK for Grosskreuzer, or "great cruiser"), differed in their speed with GK4542 having 26 boilers (16 coal-fired and 10 oil-fired) and GK4541 have two more, both oil-fired). The two ships had the same hull form, but differed in turret layout, with GK4541 having a wide space between the two after turrets to accommodate a larger turbine room.

The ship would have been the largest warship built in Germany up to that time (though larger passenger liners had been launched). She would displace 45,000 tons on a length of 240 meters and bore a superficial resemblance to the L20 battleship design and its related variants. Like them, all of her boilers were trunked into a single gigantic

Battle cruiser *Mackensen* on the slipway.

funnel, though her internal arrangements differed thanks to her much larger engine spaces.

The sea officers had asked for thicker side armor, and the new designs provided it, with substantially more protection than the previous great cruiser designs or and only slightly less than the new battleships. Like the other new ships she would have a reasonably thick armored deck, and follow the "honeycomb" pattern of internal subdivision common to German large warships.

Main armament would be eight of the new 420mm SK L/45 naval rifle, a weapon then still in the early design stage and many months from even test firing. Like most late-war German designs, she carried them in the USN Pattern, what naval writer Siegfried Breyer later described as "the peak of perfection" — in four twin turrets, two forward and two aft. Eight 150mm (5.9-inch) guns would be mounted in an armored casemate battery, with four more in high-angle anti-aircraft mounts on the main deck, arrayed on either side of turret "C." She had a single, bow-mounted torpedo tube, avoiding the difficulties of launching a torpedo from a side mount while the ship made any sort of speed (caught in the rush of water, the torpedo had a tendency to hang halfway out of the tube, creating a potential hazard).

The designers broke with earlier practice, replacing the tripod masts used on previous heavy warships with single thick, tubular masts — a feature carried over in a number of designs from the Weimar and Nazi eras.

This book's Victoria Luise class has four ships built to design GK4541, since I liked its looks better than the slightly slower version (in game terms, there is no difference in their speed). She is a powerful ship, the equal of

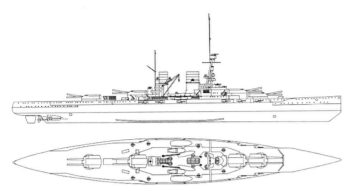

A line drawing of the *Mackensen* design.

most of the late-generation battleships in terms of firepower and protection combined with a battle cruiser's speed.

By the time her design had been finished, Imperial Germany had little hope of building new capital ships. Even had the resources been available — steel and labor, for the most part — such a massive ship would have taken at least four years to build, and possibly longer. She would not have been available for action unless the Great War dragged on for a terrible length, in which case it's unlikely that Germany would have the capability to build such a ship even if some sort of cease-fire or truce paused the carnage. More likely, she would have been built after some sort of negotiated peace that left Imperial Germany intact and capable of joining the post-war naval arms race — this is the alternative history offered in our *Second Great War* setting, where this ship appears in our CRUEL SEA expansion set.

Russian Battle Cruisers

Defeat in the Russo-Japanese War, followed by social revolution in Russian cities, had profound effects on the Imperial Russian Navy. The war's lessons would be rigorously studied, and applied to tactics, operational plans and warship design.

In one of the few Russian successes at sea, the squadron of armored cruisers based at Vladivostok had steamed around Japan, preying on merchant shipping in waters the Japanese had believed utterly safe, thereby sparking panic among both government and civilians. The Japanese armored cruiser squadron, meanwhile, had stood in the battle line alongside the actual battleships and used their speed to help bring the Russian fleet to battle on terms of Admiral Heihachiro Togo's choosing.

Starting in 1907, the Russian Naval General Staff developed its 1909-1919 fleet program with priority given to a squadron of four armored cruisers for the Baltic Fleet. These ships should have the range to operate deep in enemy waters on independent missions, the speed to screen the battle fleet and the heavy guns and armor to allow them to fight alongside the newly ordered dreadnoughts.

The Marine Technical Committee issued its initial requirements in May 1910: a speed of at least 28 knots and armament of at least eight 305mm (12-inch) guns, on a ship 204 meters long powered by turbines able to develop 80,000 horsepower. A great deal of discussion and modification included an increase in armament to at least nine 305mm guns in three triple turrets and a silhouette similar to that of the Gangut-class battleships. The requests for proposals went out to six Russian and 17 foreign shipyards in August 1911: affirming the words of V.I. Lenin, the firms invited to bid on the project included the German shipyards A.G. Vulkan and Blohm und Voss, both of which provided detailed proposals.

The Committee rejected all proposals that included superfiring turrets, strongly preferring that all turrets be sited on the main-deck level in the same "Cuniberti" arrangement as the Gangut class battleships. Blohm und Voss included a proposal for four turrets with 356mm (14-inch) guns that the committee liked so much that they apparently leaked the concept to two of the Russian competitors. The committee then chose a design by St. Petersburg's New Admiralty shipyard.

The Navy Ministry desperately wanted this ship, but she did not fall within the budgetary guidelines laid down by

Izmail prepares for launch.

the Duma in June 1912. Modifications ensued, shaving off some armor and reducing the maximum speed by a knot to 27 knots. Estimates still came in over budget, so with the aid of some bureaucratic subterfuge the missing amount came from money already approved for the Svetlana-class light cruisers, which now became somewhat slower and smaller.

With that settled, the Ministry placed formal orders in September 1912: two ships from New Admiralty (eventually named *Borodino* and *Navarin*) and two from rival Baltic (*Izmail* and *Kinburn*). Delivery was set for July 1916 for the first two ships (one from each yard) and September 1916 for the remaining pair. Work began on all four in the spring of 1913.

Problems cropped up almost immediately. Testing showed that 305mm armor-piercing rounds could easily punch through the proposed armor plate; even shots that did not penetrate shattered the backing and collapsed the upper deck. The armor would have to be thickened and its fittings reinforced, increasing the ship's weight. The new test basin turned out to have a defective engine (to gener-

Izmail hits the water.

ate waves) and a design team was sent to Germany along with their model of the ship's hull. The Germans found that the hull did not actually match its theoretical dimensions, dropping the ships' speed still further to 26.5 knots. The New Admiralty yard management blamed the German test engineers, but Russian Navy experts confirmed the findings.

After many additional meetings, the Navy Ministry issued directives that alternations could be made to the hull form and the armor scheme, particularly the backing of the armor plates, as long as these changes did not impact either the cost of the ships or their delivery dates. And so construction proceeded on what was now known to be a flawed design. And more problems piled up.

Franco-Russian Works, contracted to supply the turbines for the two New Admiralty-built ships, could not meet their delivery dates. New Admiralty therefore shifted the order for *Navarin*'s turbines to AG Vulkan. Some Russian-language sources claim that New Admiralty only ordered components from Germany, but Vulkan would later offer a complete turbine set to the German Navy and build a pair of light cruisers around the machinery. *Navarin* would be left without a power plant when war broke out with Germany. At least one other ship's propeller shafts had been ordered in Germany as well.

Baltic, which built its own turbines, could not fulfill its own needs and ordered the turbines for *Kinburn* from Parsons in England. What became of them is unclear; they don't appear to have been delivered.

Likewise, the Obukov Works, contracted to supply the heavy guns, could not meet its delivery dates and sub-con-

tracted 36 of the guns (from an order of 76 total, including spares and 18 guns intended for coast-defense batteries) to Vickers in England. Vickers in turn experienced delays in setting up production — these were Russian-designed weapons, not an off-the-shelf Vickers type — and then further delays as war broke out and orders for the British armed forces exploded while transport to Russia became exceedingly difficult. Ten Vickers-made guns finally arrived in May 1917; Obukhov only managed to produce one of their allotted 40.

Had the ships been completed, they would have been large, heavily armed, but only moderately fast, closer to fast battleships than actual battle cruisers. In addition to the dozen 14-inch guns, they would have had twenty-four 130mm (5.1-inch) guns in an unusual double-decked casemate battery. They had good armor protection on their turrets and decks, but their armored belt was significantly thinner than that of German battle cruisers but about the same as the later British battle cruisers (Lion and Tiger classes).

A Russian 305mm triple turret. The 356mm mount would have been very similar.

The inability of Russian industry to supply key components in a timely manner meant that these ships would never have been completed during the course of the Great War. Even so, work continued as did design modifications based on experience with the new Gangut-class battleships, resulting in increased funnel heights. Three ships were launched in 1915, with *Navarin* finally hitting the water in November 1916. Despite the pressing needs of the war effort, the shipyards received special dispensations for labor and materials to continue the battle cruiser projects — despite the impossibility of actually completing them.

By the time the war ended, the Russian Empire had faded away as well. The Workers' Councils demanded that construction continue in order to protect the shipyard workers' jobs, but it moved only slowly. Work finally stopped on all four by the end of 1917.

Over the following years the Bolshevik regime studied various proposals for completing the ships as designed, with twin turrets for 16-inch (406mm) guns, or finishing one of them (*Izmail*) as an aircraft carrier. None of those projects went forward — Soviet Russia was in much

Navarin and *Borodino* under construction at New Admiralty shipyard.

worse economic condition than Imperial Russia had been — and three of the hulls were sold to a German scrap dealer in 1923 with *Izmail*, the abortive aircraft carrier, hitting the breakers in 1931.

Pieces for all four ships appear in our JUTLAND game, but they get no action in the scenarios (since they were never completed, and JUTLAND is a game overwhelmingly based on actual history). We fixed that in JUTLAND 1919.

Blücher, Germany's last armored cruiser.

Fast Armored Cruisers

The German Side

In the wake of the Battle of Jutland in early June 1916, the German Admiralty immediately began to assess the performance of its ships, and how these lessons should impact design of future warships.

While most of the discussion centered on capital ships — battleships and battle cruisers — much of the fighting had been done by smaller units, the light cruisers and destroyers. As the battleship and battle cruiser types converged toward a single fast battleship category, the steady increase in size and firepower took the battle cruisers away from their original mission of providing heavy fire support to the scouting forces.

The admirals identified two tasks for their cruisers in a fleet action: to drive away enemy destroyers so they could not make torpedo attacks on the German battle line, and to drive off the enemy light cruisers that interfered with German destroyers attempting to make torpedo attacks on the enemy battle line. Light cruisers could perform the first task, but the second required a larger, more powerful warship. The armored cruiser had filled this role before being supplanted by the battle cruiser; it could carry larger guns and its greater size provided a stable gun platform in seas that rendered smaller warships unable to fire effectively. Perhaps it was time for this ship type to return.

Vice Admiral Georg Hebbinghaus, who had commanded the Second Scouting Group (light cruisers and destroyers) at Dogger Bank and Jutland, presented a series of sketches for a new type of cruiser. His preferred model would carry a mixed armament of 8.2-inch (210mm) guns to drive off enemy light cruisers, and 5.9-inch (150mm) guns to handle enemy destroyers. And it would have a lot of them: a dozen 5.9-inch guns in three quadruple turrets, and four 8.2-inch guns in a pair of double turrets. An additional dozen 5.9-inch guns would be carried in the casemate, for a total of 24 such weapons, and fourteen 4.7-inch guns in the casemate as well. His sketches also featured gigantic battle flags; about 20 meters long judging by the size of the gun turrets.

The hull would be a miniature version of the battle cruiser *Derfflinger*, considered one of the best such designs to have come off German draft tables. She would be smaller than the battle cruiser, displacing between 12,000 and 14,000 tons compared to 26,600 for *Derfflinger*, and retain the same mixed coal- and oil-fired power plant (a smaller version, of course, to fit the smaller hull) for a desired high speed (by inference 32 knots, though Hebbinghaus does not appear to have named a specific speed target).

The Admiralty committee studying new ship designs immediately had objections, some practical and some political. On the practical level, the mixed main armament of 8.2-inch and 5.9-inch guns seemed problematical, though Germany's last armored cruiser designs, *Scharnhorst* and

Blücher, had also carried a combination of the two calibers and experienced no problems in distinguishing shell splashes.

Instead some suggested two cruiser designs sharing the same hull and machinery: one armed with ten 8.2-inch guns in five twin turrets, the other with twenty 5.9-inch guns in five quadruple turrets. Apparently they intended to keep the casemate weapons as well.

The ship would displace slightly less than *Blücher*, Germany's final armored cruiser, with a narrow hull form allowed by the use of turbines and small-tube boilers rather than the reciprocating engines of *Blücher*. She would probably be armored on a scale to repel similar British armament (the 9.2-inch guns of armored cruisers) but not against heavy shellfire.

Germany's 8.2-inch gun, formally the 210mm SK L/45 rifle, was an exceptionally fine weapon; it had armed only one ship (*Blücher*) before the Germans began building great cruisers with larger guns. At maximum elevation the gun's range slightly topped that of the 12-inch Mark X that equipped the first British battle cruisers. It would have given the ship a substantial advantage in both range and striking power over British cruisers armed with Mark XII six-inch guns.

The German 150mm SK L/45 had performance almost identical to that of the British Mark XII. The new cruiser's firepower advantage would come from the massive number of tubes. Krupp had made some rough sketches for a 12-inch triple turret, but the mounting had never been built let alone tested, and a quadruple turret would have been even more complex.

A much greater problem would be the political question raised by such a ship: would she count as a scout cruiser, or a great cruiser? Her size and role implied the latter, in which case she would absorb funding intended for battle cruisers. Though Alfred von Tirpitz had been forcibly retired, he retained many acolytes within the Admiralty who did not wish to trade a 14,000-ton armored cruiser, no matter how needed or capable, for a 35,000-ton battle cruiser. Pointing out the lesser cost of the armored cruiser — allowing more of them to be built for the same cost — would only highlight the soaring price tags of the big ships.

For this book, we accepted the committee's critique of the Hebbinghaus proposal and split the design into two variants, one with 8.2-inch guns and one with 5.9-inch guns

Another view of armored cruiser *Blücher*.

— one to oppose enemy cruisers, and one to oppose enemy destroyers. The ship with larger guns would have been easier to construct, as she would use the same turrets as *Blücher* (each with its own magazine, unlike the over-complex shared-magazine arrangement in *Blücher*) and draw heavily on the *Derfflinger* design for her hull, armor and machinery layouts. The ship with smaller guns would share the latter advantages, but some of the German architects appear to have doubted that the quadruple turret could be made to work properly without a great deal of time devoted to design and testing.

Hebbinghaus had experience in naval construction as well as combat command, an unusual combination in any navy, but like many sea officers appears to have asked for too much on the allotted displacement. Enlarging the ship would simply create a weakly-armed battle cruiser, and so she would probably have had to lose some of the planned casemate guns; at least that's the solution we've taken in JUTLAND 1919. Both variants have a casemate battery of a dozen 120mm (4.7-inch) guns. Germany had no 120mm gun in service when Hebbinghaus made his proposal, but Skoda had built such a weapon for the Austro-Hungarian Navy. The Germans had adopted several larger Skoda gun designs for their drawing-board battleships including the 350mm gun that would have armed the Mackensen-class battle cruisers and the massive 420mm intended for the late-generation paper battleships, but Krupp disliked paying license fees and lobbied hard against imported artillery designs.

The British Side

Britain laid down her last true battle cruiser, *Tiger*, in the summer of 1912 and launched her in December of the following year. As construction proceeded, the Admiralty discussed what sort of warships would follow her, chiefly focusing their attention on new fast battleships that could combine the functions of a battleship and battle cruiser.

The Second Sea Lord, Sir John Jellicoe, pointed out that the growth of the battle cruiser in size, speed and fighting power not only had merged the type with the battleship, but had left its original roles unfilled. A new type of cruiser, with 9.2-inch guns and a battle cruiser's high speed, seemed necessary to protect overseas commerce from high-speed enemy raiders and to support scouting forces.

Following up on Jellicoe's points, Sir Eustace Tennyson d'Eyncourt, the Director of Naval Construction, produced some rough sketches of a ship to meet those requirements. The design he labeled E3 weighed in at just under 18,000 tons, with eight 9.2-inch guns in four double turrets — in essence, a smaller version of *Tiger*. A version without armor came in at 15,500 tons, but neither was approved for construction.

Jellicoe had waged this argument before: in 1908, as Director of Naval Ordnance, he had urged that the new battle cruiser *Indefatigable* carry 9.2-inch guns rather than 12-inch guns, arguing that battleship-sized guns were not needed to destroy enemy commerce raiders and the reduction in armament would produce a cost savings of 40 percent, allowing more ships to be built. Jellicoe had appeared to win this point until Parliament learned of the proposed change and weighed in with its opinion that British warships should never be reduced in fighting power.

And it would not be the last time Jellicoe would face this question. Almost exactly one year after the 1913 discussions, in October 1914, when he had command of the Grand Fleet, he saw his powerful battle cruisers detached to the South Atlantic and the United States' East Coast to counter German commerce raiders. The Royal Navy had no ships with both speed and range to catch armed Ger-

Gun turrets for armored cruiser *Shannon*.

man passenger liners, other than massive battle cruisers armed with heavy guns. The smaller fast armored cruisers that he had championed could have performed the same role without diminishing the fighting power of the Grand Fleet. Jellicoe bitterly opposed the removal of the battle cruisers from home waters and raged against his mentor, First Sea Lord Sir John Fisher, "to the point of insubordination" as he put it later.

In calmer temper, Jellicoe revived the notion of a fast ship with 9.2-inch guns, but by this point Britain's wartime naval program had no place for new ship designs and nothing came of his proposal.

This book's set of pieces includes the ship Jellicoe wanted, here called the Surprise class. Had they been approved in 1913 they likely would have been called the E class, but another E class appeared afterward as did a (never built) F class, so we've jumped ahead to the letter S.

Surprise follows Tennyson's sketch to a large degree and retains the Fisher "Dreadnought" concept of a single-caliber battery, in this case of 9.2-inch guns. As Jellicoe had to be aware, the 9.2-inch Mark X and Mark XI guns carried by later-model British armored cruisers and semi-dreadnoughts were very poor weapons: short-ranged, prone to wear out quickly and extraordinarily inaccurate. Equipping a new and expensive ship (even if less costly than a battle cruiser) with such a crapulent weapon would have been a terrible decision and quite unlike a gunnery expert like John Jellicoe.

And so we've posited that *Surprise* would have carried a new-model 9.2-inch gun, which would have been designated Mark XVI. Britain did not produced a really high-quality heavy naval gun until the Vickers-designed 13.5-inch Mark V, ordered in 1909 and introduced in 1912 (orders, testing and acceptance all taking place during Jellicoe's term as Director of Naval Ordnance). The Vickers-led heavy gun combine had stifled innovation, since orders (and profits) were guaranteed, but as Jellicoe drove the cruiser project, we've assumed that he would also make sure that his pet project would have a modern, effective armament.

If British technology was somewhat behind in gun design, it excelled in producing turbines. The new cruiser would be powered by Yarrow oil-fired boilers and Parsons turbines, probably giving her the same 29 knots as *Tiger*, more than enough to run down German commerce raiders and fight in the North Sea as part of the scouting forces if needed.

Jolly British tars clean the breech of a 9.2-inch gun.

The Admiralty finally answered the need for an "Atlantic Cruiser" with the Hawkins class, an enlarged light cruiser armed with six 7.5-inch guns. She would be able to out-fight the German light cruisers armed with 5.9-inch (150mm) guns; *Surprise* had been designed to tackle more formidable opponents, like the proposed German cruisers armed with 170mm (6.7-inch) or 210mm (8.2-inch) guns (the latter ship is also present in the JUTLAND 1919 mix).

Surprise would have sufficient armor to make her invulnerable to German cruiser guns (though the 210mm rounds probably could have penetrated her hide). She had been intended to make short work of German cruisers and armed merchant raiders, and anything other than an actual capital ship. Rather than an enlarged light cruiser like *Hawkins*, she represented a scaled-down battle cruiser (Tennyson projected her length at 580 feet, making her actually slightly longer than the early battle cruisers). As such, she would have been much better suited to the Dreyer fire control systems mounted on the Grand Fleet's battleships and battle cruisers starting in 1916.

We included four examples of the ship. Had four of them been present in the autumn of 1914, they would have probably eliminated the German East Asia Cruiser Squadron as effectively as Admiral Sturdee's battle cruisers, without affecting the balance of power in the North Sea. That probably would have required that they be ordered sometime before the October 1913 meetings; had they been laid down as a result of those discussions they likely would not have joined the fleet before mid-1915 at the earliest.

By that point in the war any German commerce raiders on the high seas would have been converted merchant ships, easily dealt with by the older cruisers on station. The danger would come from modern new cruisers breaking out into the Atlantic, and that would have placed the Surprise class with the Grand Fleet. There, they might easily have suffered the same fate as the First Cruiser Squadron at Jutland if poorly deployed.

But that decision's up to you. Just don't send them up against German battle cruisers.

Russian Light Cruisers

The fleet modernization program put together by the Russian Navy Ministry in the years following the Russo-Japanese War included a whole array of very modern, fast warships: battle cruisers, destroyers and light cruisers.

To fill the light cruiser role, the Russian Naval General Staff initially asked for an enlarged version of the fast cruiser *Novik*, reputedly the fastest warship in the Russian fleet. Built in Germany, *Novik* had been sunk in battle with two Japanese armored cruisers and with her light armament (six 120mm, or 4.7-inch, guns) she could do nothing to fend off the bigger enemy ships.

The new ship would also be fast, but carry 152mm (six-inch) guns and have greater size and therefore staying power. That requirement evolved, as the Naval General Staff steadily increased the size of the ship to eventually reach 10,000 tons, with varying armaments including eight 203mm (8-inch) guns in four twin turrets before settling on a dozen 152mm guns in four triple turrets. The ship would be a miniature version of the Borodino-class battle cruisers, with a silhouette to match them.

She would be powered by turbines, and make 30 knots. With her powerful armament she would have been able to overwhelm any German cruiser, and use her speed advantage to elude German armored cruisers with 210mm guns or rapidly close with them and overwhelm them with her greater rate of fire. Her size would also allow her to make use of Russian advances in gunnery direction.

Cost overruns in the battle cruiser program scuttled that design, and project director I.K. Grigorivich was ordered to cut 7 million rubles from each ship's budget of 15.3

Svetlana as completed, as the Soviet *Krasny Krim*.

million rubles, a drop of nearly half. And so the ship design had to be cut nearly in half as well: down to 6,500 tons and an armament of a fifteen 130mm (5.1-inch) guns, nine of them in single shield mounts and six in casemates. Speed would drop slightly to 29.5 knots, and the ship of course now required a smaller power plant to achieve that. Unusual for the time, a seaplane would also have been carried.

Since the ship would no longer have turrets, her silhouette would be made to look like the new *Novik*-type destroyers then also in the design phase. The massive crane for the seaplane ruined that effect, but she did have three funnels just like the destroyers. She would carry two underwater torpedo tubes amidships, and was fitted to carry and lay 100 mines. She also had four 63mm anti-aircraft guns, and four machine guns fitted for the same purpose. A three-inch-thick armored belt stretched almost her full length, with two 20mm armored decks.

The first pair (*Svetlana* and *Admiral Greig*) were laid down in July 1913 at Russo-Baltic's Reval (present-day Talinn, Estonia) shipyard, with their two sisters (*Admiral Butakov* and *Admiral Spiridov*) following in November at St. Petersburg's Putilov Works. Four near-sisters, the Admiral Nakhimov class, were ordered for the Black Sea Fleet as well.

One ship, *Svetlana*, was launched in late 1915 and the other three in 1916, but none had been completed when the revolutions brought a chaotic end to shipbuilding in 1917. *Svetlana* herself would be evacuated to Kronstadt when 85 percent complete, but would not be finished before the Tsarist government fell and she saw no action in the First World War.

Admiral Butakov and *Admiral Spiridov* under construction.

Svetlana would eventually be completed by the Bolsheviks after the war as *Profintern*; she transferred to the Black Sea Fleet in 1930. Renamed *Krasny Krim* in 1939, she survived the Great Patriotic War and was eventually decommissioned in 1958. Though some sources claim she was scrapped afterward, her hulk apparently still exists in Poti. The Bolsheviks also considered completing *Admiral Butakov*, 50 percent complete when work stopped for good. Renamed *Voroshilov*, she remained laid up in St. Petersburg (re-named Leningrad) awaiting completion for decades until she was finally noticed and scrapped in 1956.

The remaining two sisters were completed as oil tankers in 1926 (German submarine depredations caused a world-wide shipping shortage in the years following the Great War). They moved to the Black Sea, where one of them ran aground in 1938 and was declared a total loss and the other was captured by the Germans in 1941, scuttled in 1943, raised by the Soviets and used as a floating fuel depot until she was scrapped in the 1960's.

No other modern light cruisers were built for the Baltic Fleet; in 1915 a set of four fast minelaying cruisers very similar to the German *Bremse* was authorized, but no work began. Whether the Russians had knowledge of the German plans or simply drew the same conclusions from the experience of war in the Baltic isn't clear, but they would have been very useful ships and likely forced the Germans to commit a large number of their own modern cruisers to the Baltic to protect the vital ore shipments from northern Sweden.

Admiral Spiridov laid up in St. Petersburg, 1917.

Admiral Nakhimov under construction at Nikolayev's Russud shipyard, 1915.

Svetlana and her sisters would have been formidable ships as originally designed, decades ahead of their time. The Germans would have had no answer for them. As built, *Svetlana* compared well with contemporary cruisers but as the war continued she slipped into obsolescence before she was even complete. British and German light cruisers began to carry six-inch or 150mm guns with greater range and shell weight than *Svetlana*'s 130mm guns; her casemate mounts made it difficult to upgrade her armament to match. Her gunnery layout was much less efficient than that of later British light cruisers, which placed all of their guns along the centerline, but all of the German cruisers actually built shared this flaw as well. *Svetlana* still had an edge in speed, but later German cruiser designs would have eclipsed her.

As with the Borodino-class battle cruisers, the innovative design features of the light cruisers outstripped the ability of Russian industry to produce them. Russian industry underwent rapid growth in the years just before the First World War, but could not continue to produce ships once the shock of war struck, and still needed to import key components that now became unavailable.

Pieces for *Svetlana* and her sisters appear in our JUTLAND game, but as with the Borodino-class battle cruisers they see no action in that game's scenarios. That's fixed in JUTLAND 1919, where they can take on their role as scouts and screen for the battle line and as independent operators deep in German waters.

German Light Cruisers

Alfred von Tirpitz, the architect of Germany's High Seas Fleet, came up through the officer ranks as a cruiser deck officer, ship captain and finally squadron commander. Though better remembered today for his obsession with battleships as State Secretary for the Imperial Navy (the equivalent of other nations' Navy Minister), Tirpitz also supported a constant program of cruiser construction, so long as a funding stream separate from that for the battleships paid the bills.

The cruiser force faced a shortage of hulls during the years before the Great War, as Tirpitz declared battle cruisers to be "great cruisers," just like the preceding armored cruisers, and funded them under that label. But he always intended the battle cruisers to serve with the High Seas Fleet, and never on overseas stations. That shifted the burden more and more to the light cruisers, known to the Germans as "small cruisers," and the aging armored cruisers left over from the pre-dreadnought era.

Yet cruiser construction did not keep up with the needs of the expanding fleet and ongoing commitment to foreign stations. Much of this had to do with soaring costs of ever-larger capital ships; battle cruiser *Von der Tann*, laid down in 1908, cost 36.5 million gold marks while the four light cruisers laid down that year cost 32.6 million gold marks for the entire class. By 1912, the cost of the newly laid-down *Derfflinger* had risen to 56 million gold marks, while the light cruiser class laid down that year (two ships of the Graudenz class) had remained fairly constant at 8.8 million gold marks. Given the choice, Tirpitz preferred one *Derfflinger* to six or seven *Graudenzes*.

While Imperial Germany built dreadnoughts in classes of four and sometimes five ships, cruisers lagged well behind in the funding race despite a much greater need for the smaller vessels. Usually the Navy only ordered a pair of new "small cruisers" (light cruisers in other navies' parlance) in a fiscal year, and these had to be spread between the fleet's scouting forces and overseas stations.

Not until the outbreak of the First World War did the High Seas Fleet address its relative shortage of cruisers, laying down 16 hulls between 1914 and 1916 — two fast mine-laying cruisers and 14 slightly improved repeats of the last pre-war design (itself a class of only two ships).

The Last Light Cruisers

By the summer of 1916, the Imperial Navy had lost 17

Light cruiser *Cöln*, lead ship of her class.

small cruisers: *Hela* and *Undine* to British submarines; *Ariadne*, *Mainz* and *Cöln* in 1914 to British battle cruisers; *Frauenlob*, *Rostock*, *Wiesbaden* and *Elbing* at Jutland; *Bremen* to mines; *Leipzig* and *Nürnberg* at the Battle of the Falklands; *Emden* in a gun battle off Cocos Island; *Magdeburg* to grounding; *Karlsruhe* to an accidental internal explosion; and finally *Königsberg* and *Dresden* scuttled by their crews far from home. Additionally, *Breslau* had gone to Constantinople in 1914 to be "sold" to the Turks and wasn't coming back any time soon.

The outbreak of war lifted budgetary restrictions. Four cruisers had already been authorized under the 1913 appropriations, and the Imperial Navy's 1914 program included a dozen new cruisers: two fast minelayers built using turbines ordered by the Russians and seized by the Germans, and ten of the Cöln class (often referred to as the Second Cöln class). For the sake of building speed, the new class' design would be a modified version of the previous one, the Nürnberg class (similarly called the Second Nürnberg class).

The Imperial Navy had hit on a satisfactory light cruiser design with *Wiesbaden*, built under the 1912 program and laid down in 1913 with one sister ship. The 1913 program included four improved, slightly larger copies (the Second Nürnberg class). These cruisers displaced 5,400 tons, on a hull 145 meters long with a 60mm armored belt and 40mm armored deck.

Main armament consisted of eight 150mm (5.9-inch) guns, all in single mounts distributed with two forward side-by-side, two on either side in "waist" positions, and two more aft in superfiring alignment along the center line. The ships carried four 450mm torpedo tubes (in a pair of single mounts on either side) and a pair of 88mm anti-aircraft guns. The geared turbines in *Karlsruhe* produced over 50,000 horsepower, good for a speed of 29 knots.

All of that yielded a ship larger, more heavily armed and slightly faster than the British C-class light cruisers then entering the Grand Fleet. The British ships did have a superior gunnery layout, with all five of the 6-inch guns carried by the later groups of C-class cruisers positions along the centerline and able to fire on either broadside — the same number of guns as the bigger German ships.

While the British light cruisers were intended primarily for fleet service — Britain had plenty of older armored cruisers for colonial duty — the German cruisers had to serve multiple roles, and even with war upon them the Imperial Navy designed cruisers capable of service on foreign stations as well as ahead of the battle fleet. That required a bigger ship with greater range. The High Seas Fleet considered these ships a very sound design, and very successful.

The Second Cöln class kept the geared turbines of *Karlsruhe*, which vastly improved their fuel efficiency and therefore their range. The dozen boilers of the previous class, 10 of them coal-fired and two oil-fired, went to fourteen in the new ships with eight of them burning coal and six burning oil. They had the same gunnery layout as the preceding class, but swapped the 450mm torpedo tubes for more-powerful 600mm models and added a third 88mm anti-aircraft gun. All ten cruisers were to be fitted to carry and lay up to 200 mines. Like previous classes, the new cruisers had two propeller shafts and were considered highly maneuverable.

Five of the new cruisers were laid down in 1915, and five more in 1916. And then work proceeded very slowly; Germany had possessed a vibrant heavy industry sector before the outbreak of war, but performed terribly in organizing that economy for war. Factories and shipyards suffered labor shortages while at the same time farm laborers

Light cruiser *Dresden*, of the Second Cöln class.

and workers in small businesses were thrown out of work when their managers or owners were called into uniform. Unemployment rose even as the war industries desperately needed more workers, but the government had no plan to match these jobless workers with workerless jobs.

Britain laid down thirteen light cruisers in 1915 and 1916, and commissioned all of them before the end of the war. Germany laid down ten of this class, and commissioned two: *Cöln* in January 1918 and *Dresden* in March. Of the others, one (*Wiesbaden*) was five months from completion when the war ended, two of them (*Leipzig* and *Rostock*) seven months away, one (*Magdeburg*) nine months away and one (*Frauenlob*) thirteen months away. The remaining three were never launched. The A.G. Vulkan shipyard in Stettin did complete the two cruisers of the Brummer class also laid down in 19195 relatively quickly, as they did not need their turbines manufactured, and both saw considerable action before war's end. Neither of the new cruisers of the Second Cöln class assigned to A.G. Vulkan would be commissioned.

Cöln and *Dresden* both took part in the High Seas Fleet's last sortie, in April 1918, and both were slated to play a major role in the abortive October 1918 attack on the Thames estuary. Their crews remained loyal to the fleet command during the Sailors' Revolt, with *Dresden*'s crew scuttling the ship rather than turn her over to the rebels. She was raised and given slap-dash repairs, and both cruisers went to Scapa Flow to be interned after the Armistice and were scuttled there, where their wrecks remain. Their eight sister ships would all be scrapped over the next several years.

New Designs

As the German Admiralty met to discuss new warship types, they gave most of their attention to heavy warships, but found time to study a new light cruiser as well.

The debate over a new cruiser centered on whether the Navy should build one multi-purpose type, or separate colonial cruisers and fleet cruisers. The fleet cruisers would be smaller, faster, and heavily-armed for their size (five 150mm guns and four torpedo tubes); Kaiser Wilhelm II personally requested such a proposal, modeled on the Royal Navy's C-class small cruisers.

The bigger cruisers followed the same basic layout as the last class of light cruisers, displacing up to twice as much as the smaller designs but offering greater range and more guns for the larger variants. They would remain dual-purpose ships, suitable for service in the Navy's far-flung

Light cruiser *Frankfurt*, of the Wiesbaden class, as an American target ship.

colonial squadrons but also with the High Seas Fleet's scouting forces. Most of the extra space went for better crew accommodations; sailors serving aboard the smaller cruisers would live on barracks ashore when the High Seas Fleet was not actually at sea. The bigger cruisers would also, of course, cost more than the smaller ships.

The admirals also looked at variations of the larger light cruisers armed with heavier guns, 170mm (6.7-inch) guns and the excellent 210mm (8.2-inch) SK L/45 rifle that armed the ill-fated armored cruiser *Blücher* and the fast armored cruiser proposed by Vice Admiral Georg Hebbinghaus.

While the 210mm gun might seem an overly large weapon for a light cruiser, the British certainly feared that such a ship was under construction and ordered their Hawkins class cruisers to counter it. At 170 meters the cruiser designed to carry the weapon was longer than *Blücher* though considerably narrower, and the big guns would have been placed in shielded single mounts rather than turrets, with four such weapons all along the centerline (in place of eight 150mm guns). These proposals appear to have had little support; the admirals preferred keeping a uniform main armament across their cruiser force.

Both the fleet cruiser and the larger cruiser would have nominal deck and belt armor, little changed from previous classes. The bigger ship could make 31 knots and the smaller one 33 knots (though a variation on the design made 30 knots at a considerable decrease in horsepower); all of the designs featured dual coal- and oil-burning power plants driving geared turbines. All of the design variants carried four above-water torpedo tubes in train-

able deck mounts; some had four single mounts and others two dual mounts. Unusually for German cruiser designs, most of the proposals were not fitted for minelaying.

Both cruisers represented an upgrade over the previous Cöln class, which could only had a designed speed of 27 knots (though the two ships completed hit 29 knots on trials). The Cöln class had exactly double the estimated range of the new, smaller fleet cruiser and a heavier gun armament, but like other German light cruisers could not operate alongside German destroyers without slowing them down. The new ship gave the Scouting Forces a cruiser that could accompany the destroyers into battle and lend them her heavier gunnery support.

The mission requirement for the larger ship is less clear; she had the speed of her smaller cousin but the heavier rate of fire afforded by more, smaller main guns would have been more useful to the Scouting Forces than the bigger guns despite their much greater effective range. The big guns would have been useful for engaging enemy cruisers outside their own envelope, but the fast armored cruiser proposed by Hebbinghaus would have filled that role far more effectively. This would have come at a much greater cost, but the admirals don't seem to have been overly concerned about the taxpayers' gold marks.

The Pieces

We included all seven of the Second Cöln class ships actually launched in our JUTLAND game, and the three scrapped on the slip are in this book's set of pieces. The ships in JUTLAND bear the names they were assigned. German practice did not grant an actual name to a ship until it had been launched, and so those in this book have been given the names of German cities in keeping with the usual practice; one (*Bremen*) carries the name of a sunken light cruiser and surely would have been used for one of them.

This book also includes two examples of the proposed small fleet cruiser and three of the larger ship with 210mm guns. The small cruiser design has appeared before, in our out-of-print U.S. NAVY PLAN GOLD game in the colors of the Weimar Republic; we've given her a nicer drawing and of course put her in the livery of the High Seas Fleet. The bigger cruiser received little attention during the discussions, as the admirals immediately realized her limited usefulness, but she makes for an interesting game piece so we included her in the book.

Newer, Larger German Destroyers

Imperial Germany's High Seas Fleet, despite its name, was never really intended to operate on the high seas. Ship design focused on vessels capable of operating in the North Sea against the Royal Navy — resulting in a fleet that would pose a dire threat to British naval supremacy, but would be incapable of projecting power much beyond home waters. Battleships lacked crew quarters suitable for long voyages; the sailors lived in barracks while the fleet stood and anchor, and slept in hammocks slung near their duty stations on the rare occasions when they went to sea. And destroyers — styled "high seas torpedo boats" in German naval parlance — were usually much smaller than their British counterparts.

That attitude changed with the outbreak of war in August 1914 and the cancellation of Russian contracts with the German firm of AG Vulkan for turbines to power a battle cruiser and four destroyers. The German Admiralty approved Vulkan's suggestion to put the machinery into new ships for the High Seas Fleet; a pair of fast minelaying cruisers made use of the huge battle cruiser turbines (half of them fitted in each ship) and destroyers based on the Russian plans handed over to Vulkan would use the destroyer turbines.

Practical experience showed that these larger destroyers with higher freeboard to be much more useful warships than the smaller torpedo boats, but they still fell well short of British standards for seakeeping. Early war experience also showed the 88mm (3.45-inch) guns carried by German torpedo boats to be completely inadequate compared to the 4-inch (102mm) weapons of British boats. The Germans responded by re-arming their torpedo boats with 105mm (4.1-inch) guns that matched British performance, but the admirals demanded something better than their enemies' weapons.

The answer would be the truly gigantic, cruiser-sized Type 1916 Torpedo Boat (the vessel, despite its size, would still be a "torpedo boat"). Where the standard German torpedo boat (the Type 1913, also known as the V25/S49 classes) displaced 975 tons, the new boat would weigh in at 2,345 tons, nearly two and a half times heavier than the previous "large torpedo boat" and grow in length from 78 to 106 meters.

This vast increase in size would permit fitting of a new main armament to give the boats a decisive edge over British destroyers: four of the 150mm (5.9-inch) SK/L45 guns that equipped German light cruisers and served as secondary guns on most battleships and battle cruisers. The gun had enormously more range than the British 4-inch Mark IV (16,000 yards vs. 9,000 yards) while tossing a shell three times as large (45 kilograms (99 pounds) vs. 14 kilograms (31 pounds)). But that huge round could no longer be handled by one man, and so the main armament's rate of fire dropped by about a half to two-thirds, from 15 rounds per minute for the 105mm to five to seven rounds per minute for the bigger gun.

The Germans had similarly re-armed their older light cruisers, replacing their 105mm guns with the bigger 150mm. But these ships filled a different role, and were expected to stand off and support the torpedo boats with their gunfire. A cruiser-sized gun did not fit the torpedo boat's mission.

Alongside the larger guns, the new torpedo boat would mount four of the new 60cm torpedo tubes in place of the 50cm weapons previously carried. Range at top speed for the new torpedo jumped from 4,000 meters to 6,000 meters, and the explosive warhead increased slightly from 195 kilograms (430 pounds) to 210 kilograms (463 pounds). She could also carry and lay 40 mines.

SMS S113, before handing over to the French.

The 150mm SK L/45, seen here on light cruiser *Frankfurt*.

The resulting boat — despite her size, she was still considered a "boat" — had enough freeboard to allow her weapons to be served in much worse weather than had been possible for her smaller predecessors. She had great speed (34 knots), significantly faster than the V25 class, and much better range than earlier German torpedo boats.

The Navy ordered a dozen of the big torpedo boats in 1916, three each at the Schichau, Vulkan, Germaniawerft and Blohm & Voss yards. Like other German torpedo boats, they carried an alpha-numeric designation indicating their yard of manufacture: S113-S115, V116-V118, G119-G121, and B122-B124.

Only two of the huge torpedo boats would be completed, neither in time to see service with the High Seas Fleet. All of the others were broken up while still incomplete, none of them having been launched or advanced any more than 75 percent of the way to completion.

V116 was commissioned at the end of July 1918, but saw no action under the Imperial flag. After brief service in the Weimar Republic's Reichsmarine she was transferred to Italy as a war reparation and served until 1937 as Premuda. S113 was completed in August 1919 and likewise spent a brief period in the Reichsmarine before going to France as *Amiral Senes*. The other ten would be scrapped incomplete.

The two surviving boats appear to have been very successful, serving their new owners for nearly 20 years despite being one-off vessels in each fleet (though part of this no doubt related to their status as prizes of war, and therefore symbolic of the victory over Imperial Germany).

The bigger hull made them very durable and very steady at sea, but the heavy armament was probably not worth the vastly reduced rate of fire. The following Type 1918 Large Torpedo Boat reverted to the 105mm gun and 50cm torpedo tube, but was a much larger boat if not as gigantic as the Type 1916 (1,500 tons' displacement and 92 meters long).

We included seven of the huge boats in GREAT WAR AT SEA: JUTLAND, and the remaining five appear in this book. JUTLAND had no scenarios for them; we fixed that oversight here. In a melee with other destroyers their additional size is an advantage (they're harder to sink) but players would probably rather have two tertiary gunnery factors in place of the one secondary factor. They're more like under-armed cruisers than true destroyers, but without the staying power or range. Had they been given a dual 105mm mount in place of the single 150mm, they would have been formidable surface warships and a great addition to the German scouting forces. As designed and built, their heavy guns would have added much less to the High Seas Fleet's fighting power than the German Admiralty hoped.

Alongside the gigantic Type 1916 High Seas Torpedo Boat, German naval architects also drew up plans for a similar, merely large boat.

The Type 1918Mob (Mobilisierung, or "Mobilization") would serve as divisionstorpedoboote, or battle fleet destroyers, delivering torpedo attacks on the enemy battle line while the bigger Type 1916 fended off enemy destroyers with its heavy guns to clear the way. That would require a great many of the new boats, and the Imperial Navy ordered 53 of them: 32 under the 1917 appropriations, and 21 more under the 1918 fiscal year.

As they had done with the big Type 1916 torpedo boat, the architects drew heavily on the plans for the Russian Novik-class large destroyers that had naïvely been supplied by Russian shipyards looking to buy turbines from German manufacturers before the Great War's outbreak. *Novik* was faster, larger and more heavily armed than the destroyers serving other nations; Germany in particular stood behind the curve with smaller vessels — "torpedo boats" in the Imperial Navy's vernacular — than those of most other countries.

The new German torpedo boat had a layout and hull form much like that of its *Novik*-derived larger cousin, displacing just over 1,500 tons with a length of 92 meters. That came in much smaller than the huge Type 1916's 2,300

German torpedo boats in American hands post-war. From left, V43 (Type 1913); G102 (ex-Argentine destroyer *San Luis*, taken over during construction); S132 (Type 1916Mob); American minesweeper *Redwing*.

tons and 105 meters, but represented a substantial increase over the previous standard battle fleet torpedo boats. The Type 1913 had weighed in at 975 tons with a length of 78 meters and the Type 1916Mob, a somewhat improved version, at 1,100 tons and 82 meters.

The new Type 1918Mob would carry four 105mm (4.1-inch) guns, a major upgrade over the three 88mm (3.45-inch) guns of the Type 1913 (many of the Type 1913 torpedo boats had their guns replaced with 105mm pieces during the course of the war; the Type 1916Mob carried three of them from the start). Like the earlier boats, the new Type 1916Mob had six torpedo tubes: two dual mounts on the centerline, and one single mount on either side of the bridge. She was also to be fitted to carry and lay 40 mines, a substantial increase over the earlier models.

The bigger hull gave the Type 1918Mob a steadier gun platform for the heavier artillery, and much better sea-keeping in the rough waters of the North Sea. German torpedo boats had improved as high-seas warships since the earliest classes, but even the more recent versions still wallowed in heavier seas to a much greater extent than their British counterparts. The Type 1918Mob was intended to give the High Seas Fleet a destroyer that could

match British performance, allowing the battle fleet to remain at sea in the same conditions as the enemy.

The new torpedo boat was the first German destroyer-sized ship with geared turbines; she had half again the power output of the previous types — 38,000 horsepower compared to 26,000 — and therefore considerably more speed (35 knots, compared to 32 knots for earlier torpedo boats). By comparison the new light cruisers *Brummer* and *Bremse*, also equipped with geared turbines, developed 42,000 horsepower on a displacement four times that of the new torpedo boat, but only made 28 knots. The geared turbines gave the new torpedo boats much greater range than the earlier vessels, allowing them to steam much more economically at cruising speed.

All of those additional capabilities came at a price that the German Admiralty had not wished to pay in earlier years. The new, larger boats would likely have been less maneuverable than the smaller types the Germans had favored; battle experience showed that this feature did not matter so much in fleet actions, but did in close coastal waters. In response, the German Navy built a series of much smaller coastal torpedo boats to fill that role.

The new torpedo boat also had a much larger crew than the old, 117 men for the Type 1918Mob compared to 85 for the Type 1913. Alfred von Tirpitz had been firm in his desire that a torpedo boat remain small enough that her crew could be commanded by a single officer, thereby holding down the number of officers needed by the torpedo branch. That would no longer be possible with the larger boats, at least doubling the number of sea officers required. Torpedo-boat duty was considered more exciting and more likely to advance one's career — a very junior officer could command his own ship, even though it was small — and the boats siphoned off some of the Navy's most ambitious and capable young officers, annoying Tirpitz.

Of the first 32 boats ordered, 30 began construction in 1918 and two were never begun. Contracts for the 21 authorized for the 1918 fiscal year were placed, but none of the boats began construction before the war — and the Imperial government responsible for paying the bills — ended.

By the time construction began, German industry faced crippling shortages of raw materials including high grade steel and of labor. Shipyards employed fewer female workers than did munitions factories, and even a program to furlough soldiers from the front to spend time in vital

Another view of S132, of the Type 1916(Mob).

industries did not ease the problem. And so shipyards strained to build new submarines to feed the needs of unrestricted undersea warfare, and to service and repair the existing warships now feeling the strain of four years of wartime use.

Unable to fulfill its obligations in that economic environment, Howaldtswerke of Kiel, entrusted with contracts for half of the initial order, even sub-contracted four of them to Stettiner Oderwerke, a tiny shipyard previously only

known for building tugboats, river craft and small seaside excursion steamers. Oderwerke proved unable to finish them, either.

None of the boats laid down would be completed as warships; thanks to the huge post-war shortage of merchant shipping two were completed as four-masted sailing ships and two more as steam-powered coastal freighters.

As a warship design, the Type 1918Mob was similar to the fleet destroyers built by other maritime powers at the end of the Great War. The American "four-stack" destroyers were smaller (1,100 tons) with the same main gun armament but twice as many torpedo tubes. The British W-class likewise came in a little smaller than the German boats, with four 4-inch guns and six torpedo tubes.

The Type 1918Mob torpedo boat appears in this book as the V170 class destroyer; the Imperial German Navy also used the same designation system for its minesweepers ("Type" and year of design) so we needed to use something else for the destroyers.

Britain's W-Class Destroyers

As the Great War continued at sea, the Royal Navy found itself dissatisfied with its standard destroyer designs. The type had evolved rapidly over the previous decade, as torpedo boat and torpedo-boat destroyer types had merged and the size of the boats steadily increased.

In 1910 the Admiralty had issued a tender for a new oil-fueled destroyer, armed with two four-inch guns, one 12-pounder (76mm) gun and two torpedo tubes. She would displace just under 800 tons, and make a top speed of 27 knots. Over the next six years the British retained the same basic design, but continued to enlarge it and by 1916 the standard destroyer had grown to 1,000 tons, with a third four-inch gun in place of the useless 12-pounder and a second pair of torpedo tubes, and a top speed now expected to touch 32 knots.

Waterhen, a W-class destroyer in Australian service, seen between the wars.

Even the enlarged destroyer failed to keep up with the emerging needs of the war at sea: a multi-role warship able to conduct torpedo attacks, anti-submarine warfare, battle fleet screening, convoy escort, mine-laying and even more tasks. By the 1930s naval literature would describe the destroyer as a "maid of all work."

The cramped destroyers could not accommodate the extra personnel and communications gear required by a flotilla commander and his staff. To solve that problem, the Royal Navy ordered a series of destroyer leaders, enlarged versions of the destroyers with a fourth four-inch gun. The five boats ordered in April 1916, known as the V class since all five had names beginning with the letter "V," weighed in at 1,100 tons' displacement and could make 34 knots.

The new leaders made a very good impression as soon as they came off the drawing boards, causing the Admiralty

to re-think its plans to repeat the last Admiralty design. Instead they ordered 26 more units to the V-leader design, as the V-class (all with names beginning with the letter V). Though nearly identical to the destroyer leaders (they lacked the compass platform of the first group), they would serve as flotilla destroyers.

The new boats were much larger than the Admiralty standard, 312 feet long compared to 276 feet for the earlier boats. Both types carried the same machinery outfit: three oil-fired boilers powering a set of geared turbines to produce 27,000 horsepower. That gave the smaller destroyers a top speed of 36 knots, compared to 34 knots for the V-class and W-class. They carried their guns in single mounts fitted in two super-firing pairs, fore and aft, with the torpedo tubes in two banks amidships, in what became the standard British destroyer layout for the next two decades.

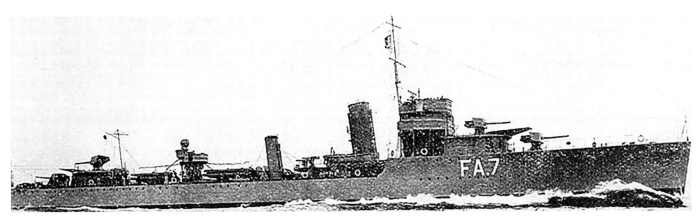

Whitshed, a Modified W-class destroyer.

Loading a torpedo aboard *Vanoc*, between the wars.

Rear Admiral Sir Morgan Singer, the Director of Naval Ordnance and Torpedoes, urged a move from dual to triple torpedo tubes, arguing that the bigger boats could easily accommodate the increased weight. Rather than delay delivery of the new destroyers, they received the same dual mounts as previous boats, but the decks beneath them were strengthened to allow the triple tubes to be fitted later if desired.

Singer's desired torpedo mounts were ready by December 1916, when the Admiralty ordered 23 more boats to the same design, and these became the W class. Other than carrying six rather than four tubes, they were identical to the V class.

In February 1917 the Admiralty decided to revert to a smaller destroyer design, opting to place what ultimately became 57 orders for S-class destroyers, a modified version of the last "Admiralty" class. These would be cheaper to build and could be commissioned more quickly, both of these serious considerations with German submarines ravaging British commerce, and were also faster at 36 knots.

But even as British shipyards laid down the smaller destroyers, the first of the larger boats ordered in the previous year began to join the fleet. Initial impressions were very positive, and the Admiralty moved to the W class for

its 1918 orders, with 16 contracts placed in January and 38 more in March and April.

The Admiralty had not finished with improvements. The bigger destroyers could mount bigger guns, and rumors of new German destroyers under construction with larger guns filtered in from various sources. The new destroyers therefore would carry the 4.7-inch guns previously mounted on the even bigger Shakespeare-class destroyer leaders. These threw a much larger shell (50 pounds, compared to 31 for the 4-inch Mark V) over a much greater distance (15,800 yards for the new weapon against 9,600 yards for the 4-inch gun).

The 4.7-inch Mark I was an outstanding weapon, able to match the range of the German 5.9-inch (150mm) gun fitted to the High Seas Fleet's new gigantic torpedo boats though not the throw-weight (its shell was just slightly more than half the weight of the 150mm round, and rate of fire was about the same). The British seem to have only been aware that the Germans had moved to larger guns, and not known of their seemingly insane decision to go with cruiser-sized weapons.

None of these "Modified W" class would see action in the Great War; sixteen of them were completed after the end of the war. They and their near-sisters became the back-

W-class *Wolfhound* (foreground) and *Wessex*, seen at Gydnia, Poland, in 1932.

bone of the post-war destroyer force, as the smaller boats were retired or scrapped. Some Modified-W boats remained in front-line service as fleet destroyers in the early months of World War II. Twenty-one others were modified for long-range escort duty, losing one boiler, two of their guns and their torpedo tubes in exchange for greater fuel bunkerage, anti-aircraft and anti-submarine weapons, and radar. Another fourteen boats would be converted to anti-aircraft escorts, and a dozen more became short-range escorts with much less extensive modifications due to wartime priorities.

In *Great War at Sea* games, the V class doesn't rate a different playing piece than the Admiralty-type destroyers; *Great War at Sea* is primarily a battleship game and there's not a lot of granularity possible when rating the smaller warships. The Modified W class appears in JUTLAND, with more of them in this book to allow the Allied player to fit out the Grand Fleet exclusively with the new boats. They have a stronger torpedo armament, with half again as many tubes per boat, but all other game ratings are the same as the Admiralty type; the 4.7-inch gun still falls within the nominal "1" rating for light guns.

Avalanche Press™, Ltd.

1820 1st Ave. S., Suite H
Irondale, AL 35210

www.AvalanchePress.com